MAPPING MACEDONIA

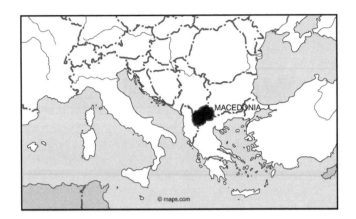

The Republic of Macedonia

MAPPING MACEDONIA

IDEA AND IDENTITY

P. H. LIOTTA AND CINDY R. JEBB

 PRAEGER

Westport, Connecticut
London

Library of Congress Cataloging-in-Publication Data

Liotta, P. H.
    Mapping Macedonia: idea and identity / P. H. Liotta, and Cindy R. Jebb.
    p. cm.
    Includes bibliographical references and index.
    ISBN 0-275-98247-5 (alk. paper)
    1. Macedonia (Republic)—Politics and government—1992- 2. Macedonia (Republic)—
    Ethnic relations—Political aspects.   3. Macedonian question.   4. Balkan Peninsula—
    Politics and government—1989-   I. Jebb, Cindy R., 1960-   II. Title.
    DR2253.L56 2004
    949.7603—dc22   2004045162

British Library Cataloguing in Publication Data is available.

Library of Congress Catalog Card Number: 2004045162
ISBN: 0-275-98247-5

First published in 2004

Praeger Publishers, 88 Post Road West, Westport, CT 06881
An imprint of Greenwood Publishing Group, Inc.
www.praeger.com

Printed in the United States of America

10 9 8 7 6 5 4 3 2 1

Copyright Acknowledgments

The authors and publisher gratefully acknowledge permission to use the following material:

An earlier version of Chapter 1 appears in P. H. Liotta, *Dismembering the State: The Death of Yugoslavia and Why It Matters* (Lanham, MD: Lexington Books, 2001).

Interviews with Kiro Gligorov and Boris Trajkovski.

E-mail addendum (July 16, 2002) to a paper written by Mark Dickinson while in residency at the Weatherhead Center for International Affairs, Harvard University.

for our students

They make a desolation and they call it peace.

—Tacitus, *Agricola*

Contents

Acknowledgments

Sections of this manuscript previously appeared in English and Macedonian in *Journal of Conflict Studies, Parameters, Problems of Post-Communism, Mediterranean Quarterly, Наше Писмо* [Our Writing], *Нова Балканска Политика* [New Balkan Politics], *Security Dialogue,* and *European Security.* An earlier version of the chapter "The Last Best Hope" appeared under a different title in *Dismembering the State: The Death of Yugoslavia and Why It Matters* (Lexington Books) and is used here with permission. Presentations and lectures that influenced these essays were made at the Woodrow Wilson International Center for Scholars (East European Studies Program), the United States Department of State, the Pan-European International Relations Conference (Vienna, 1998; Canterbury, 2001), the summit of the International Peace Research Association in Tampere, Finland, the European Union Security Institute in Paris, a joint ministerial of the WEU-Mediterranean Dialogue in Lisbon, the Mackinder Studies Group at the U.S. Naval War College, the United States Military Academy at West Point, International Studies Association meetings in New Orleans and Budapeşt; on behalf of the Center for Hemispheric Defense Studies, Brasilia, Brazil; during symposia at Complutense University and at the NATO Advanced

Research Workshop Environmental Conference in Madrid; and partially formed the basis for an advanced research project at the U.S. Naval War College.

In conducting research for this work, the authors received access to government officials, intellectuals, and civic leaders during the administrations of both President Kiro Gligorov and President Boris Trajkovski. We are especially grateful to the National Security Council of the Republic of Macedonia. Specific thanks go to Keith Brown, the Watson Institute for International Studies, Brown University; Mark Dickinson, British Ambassador to the Republic of Macedonia from 1997–2001, local representative of the Swedish EU Presidency, and the Special Representative of the European Union's High Representative for Common Foreign and Security Policy; Vladimir Čupeski; Nikola Dimitrov (former national security advisor and current Macedonian Ambassador to the United States); Liljana Dirjan; Ljubomir Frčkovski; Bogomil Gjuzel; Gjorge Ivanov; Mirjana Maleska; Macedonian National Security Advisor Stevo Pendarovksi; and Biljana Vankovska.

The views expressed here are those of the authors and do not purport to reflect the position of the United States Military Academy, the Department of the Army, or the Department of Defense.

Introduction

In 1996, the first U.S. ambassador to the Republic of Macedonia toured a household appliance factory soon after his arrival in country. Five years after the nation's independence from the former Yugoslavia, the factory's director asked the ambassador, "Do you think we will make it?" The factory, located in the poorest of the former Yugoslav republics, was a decrepit monstrosity designed to service the now lost Yugoslav market and was one of at least a dozen in Macedonia that the World Bank had insisted be either closed permanently or sold. As the ambassador stepped into the courtyard, he responded gently, "Well, if you get that electrical motor contract in Turkey. . . ." The factory director interrupted to correct the misunderstanding: "No," he said, "I mean the country. Do you think Macedonia will make it?"

In some ways, the more perverse response would *still* have been, however, "Well, if you get that electrical motor contract in Turkey. . . ." To be sure, Macedonia's precarious existence ever since its declaration of independence in 1991 has been based on conditions—political, ethnic, social, economic—that extend from outside its borders as much as internal dynamics. While Macedonia is seemingly well understood as a precarious example of potential

Balkan instability, the tiniest nation in southeast Europe is also a poorly understood success. In the broadest terms, Macedonia is characterized in the "West" as a nation where nationalist parties, the so-called Internal Macedonian Revolutionary Organization (VMRO), as well as the Social Democrats (or SDSM), at times suppressed the Albanian minority and aggravated tensions between ethnic Albanians and Slavic Macedonians. When the VMRO was not in power, the SDSM (comprised largely of former Yugoslav socialists) alternately controlled the power politics of Macedonia.

Both these portrayals were far too simplistic, of course—but the *perception* of the West was (and is), unfortunately, far more important than reality. And the challenge to reverse this perception may well represent the major security issue for Macedonia in the future.

During our research on and travel in Macedonia for this book, we have been constantly reminded, for example, of how ignorant Americans and Europeans are about the country and the Balkans in general. A perhaps frivolous example from "pop" history might best illustrate this ignorance. In 2000, a popular television game show in the United States posed as its prizewinning question the following: "Boris Trajkovski was recently elected as president of what southeast European nation?" None of the game contestants answered the question correctly; none of them, in truth, even bothered to hazard a guess.

Yet Macedonia seems, in many ways, the most shining and positive example to rise from the ashes of former Yugoslavia. Despite the obvious evidence to the contrary, reports of Macedonia's death have been greatly exaggerated. The challenges to accentuate the positive, and *deal* with the negative, will remain over coming years.

The four essays and accompanying appendices in this work offer an introduction to both the complexity and richness of this extraordinary nation-state. In conducting research for this work, the authors received unprecedented access to government officials, intellectuals, and civic leaders. We emphasize that this access proved essential to our observations and conclusions.

We thus realize, with some irony, both how blessed and how cursed the Republic of Macedonia has remained since independence. On the one hand, this tiny nation-state escaped, narrowly perhaps, the vicious cycles of destruction that consumed Croatia in 1991,

Bosnia in 1992, Kosovo in 1999, and to some extent never relented in the continuing self-destruction of Serbs and Serbia throughout the last decade of the twentieth century. On the other hand, Macedonia has had to suffer through benign and intentional neglect from both Balkan neighbors and the so-called international community ever since its 1991 declaration of independence. In 2001, with the rise of an indigenous insurgency, Macedonia came precariously close to all-out civil war.

Slighted with the label of the "Former Yugoslav Republic of Macedonia" from the earliest days of its existence, this state has managed to achieve small measures of political, social, economic, and even interethnic integration. In the Balkans—or in the wider and more euphemistic context of southeast Europe by which the Balkans is commonly known—this seems a near impossibility. Unlike Bosnia or Kosovo, Macedonia has received little infrastructure support or massive international assistance. Equally, bloodshed in the form of wide-scale, sustained conflict and ethnic cleansing has not yet happened.

On more than one occasion, Macedonia has come perilously close to collapse. Aside from a failure to complete secure resolution with Greece over various disputes (most especially the name of Macedonia for the state itself), its internal commitments to economic reform were never fully committed to during the 1990s. Further, geographical isolation, obvious lack of technological sophistication as well as lack of access to technology, and evident and continuing political instability—severely aggravated by the Kosovo crisis of 1999—failed to encourage foreign investment over the long run. That said, such investments along with the successful implementation of economic reforms are the only means to secure stability or ensure Macedonia's long-term success.

If one were to consider the Balkans over the last decade of the twentieth century and the first decade of the twenty-first century, it might indeed seem miraculous that Macedonia had not suffered a fate similar to that of its neighbors. The future for Macedonia remains laced with promise as much as peril. One evident conclusion is that the tensions between Slavic Macedonians and ethnic Albanians would continue at either an aggravated level of contest or at a manageable level to achieve workable consensus. The solution, nonetheless, could only be achieved by the peoples of the region itself. Such evidence should become a viable marker for other troubled nations of the region.

It was a tragic blow to Macedonia—and to the Balkans—when President Boris Trajkovski was killed in a plane crash in Bosnia-Herzegovina on 26 February 2004. Himself enroute to a Balkan unity summit, Trajkovski had also sent a delegation to Ireland that same day to submit Macedonia's formal application for European Union membership. Yet, even as Macedonia's story is unique among the states created out of the ruins of former Yugoslavia, there remain similarities and themes that may well repeat themselves as we witness the map of Eurasia being redrawn in what we call the 12 September era.

While the related essays in this book offer no definitive conclusion—other than to emphasize that the citizens of Macedonia will experience any number of hardships in the coming years—we do offer recommendations and possible solutions based on decades of involvement with and commitment to the region. We hope, then, that what we offer here might prove worth pondering.

The Last Best Hope: The "Future" Republic of Macedonia (A Retrospective, 1991–1999)

> The Macedonian question has been the cause of every great European war for the last fifty years, and until that is settled there will be no more peace either in the Balkans or out of them. Macedonia is the most frightful mix-up of races ever imagined. Turks, Albanians, Greeks and Bulgarians live there side by side without mingling—and have lived so since the days of St. Paul.
> —*John Reed*, The War in Eastern Europe, *1916*

One realizes with some irony both how blessed and how cursed the Republic of Macedonia remained throughout the 1990s. On the one hand, this tiny nation-state escaped, narrowly perhaps, the vicious cycles of destruction that consumed Croatia in 1991, Bosnia in 1992, Kosovo in 1999, and to some extent never relented in the continuing self-destruction of Serbs and Serbia throughout the last decade of the twentieth century. On the other hand, Macedonia had to suffer through benign and intentional neglect from both Balkan neighbors and the so-called international community since its 1991 declaration of independence.

Slighted with the label of the "Former Yugoslav Republic of Macedonia" from the earliest days of its existence, this state, the poorest of the six former republics during the nearly five decades of

Tito's Yugoslavia, managed to achieve small measures of political, social, economic, and even interethnic integration. In the Balkans, of all places, this seemed a near impossibility. Unlike Bosnia, Macedonia received little infrastructure support or massive international assistance. Equally, bloodshed in the form of conflict outbreak and ethnic cleansing on a large scale did not occur in the region (until 2001).

Until 1999, again unlike Bosnia, the presence of United Nations (UN) forces in the area paled in comparison to the wide latitude of authority and responsiveness that NATO and Stabilization Forces (S-FOR) exercised in post-Dayton Bosnia. The Balkan Stability Pact—known more formally as the Stability Pact for South Eastern Europe—signed by Macedonia in June 1999, provided the opportunity for both economic and significant material assistance to this struggling nation. The pact thus provides a measure of hope, however small, for the future Republic of Macedonia. The sad irony, of course, is that it took war in Kosovo before renewed assistance would be offered in any significant amount to Macedonia. As with Bosnia, the tragedy of a neighbor's agony provided another form of salvation both for the Macedonian people and for its continued existence as a state.

Predictions in the Balkans, even more so than elsewhere, are a foolish enterprise. A review of the various geographic and geopolitical influences should reveal, however, that conflicting and often competing political, economic, social, cultural, and historic factors will continue to vie for attention and authority. Indeed, the absence of increased attention and support to integrate Macedonia within the fold of Europe suggests that this tiny nation-state's future is more precarious than it ought to be, given the record of continued Yugoslav disintegration that preceded it during the 1990s and the attempts to prevent further disintegration.

GROUND BETWEEN FOUR NEIGHBORS: ALBANIA, BULGARIA, GREECE, AND SERBIA

The Dynamic from 1991 to 1995

Macedonia shares with Serbia the unfortunate quality of being a landlocked country. Unlike Serbia, which had an outlet to the Montenegrin port of Bar within its tenuous federation known as the Federal Republic of Yugoslavia, Macedonia has no official economic linkages to a seaport.[1] Thus, a comment made to one of the authors in private correspondence reveals an essential truth of Macedonia's current conundrum: "[T]hings are happening very fast around us (Bulgaria, Albania, Serbia . . .), between the extremes of crypto-communists and (not so crypto) nationalists. We are in danger of being ground between these millstones (each turning and accelerating in opposite directions)."[2] The tensions that divided the Macedonian nation were as much external geographic realities as internal political divisions. These tensions appeared to drive both policy decisions and Macedonia's foreign relations impasse in the region from 1991 to 1995.

The potential for economic linkages through the development of a major east-west highway that links Bulgaria, Macedonia, and Albania does exist, however; this route roughly follows the ancient Roman trade route known as the Via Egnatia.[3] Such a linkage would provide both an Albanian outlet to the Adriatic Sea for Macedonia and open a trade route to the Bulgarian ports of Varna and Burgas on the Black Sea.[4] Turkey would also have direct access to south-eastern Europe trade connections that would bypass the port of Thessaloniki in Greek Macedonia, a major shipping point on the Mediterranean.

Given the historic enmity between Greece and Turkey, such a trade route seemed desirable for Turkey to make significant inroads in an economic linkage that could potentially mix Muslim nations (Albania, Turkey, western Macedonia) with largely Orthodox nations (Bulgaria and central and eastern Macedonia). This linkage could also lead to inevitable defensive alliances, most especially between Macedonia and Albania. Again, due largely to the mistrust and enmity displayed between these Balkan neighbors from 1991 to 1995, specific and conflicting interests interfered with making this alliance a likely probability.

Albania

The tiny state of Albania, itself the poorest nation in Europe, may have (in the ideal sense) harbored designs for the western half of Macedonia. Claiming that Macedonian Albanians constitute as much as 40 percent of the Macedonian population of just over two million, Albania privately insisted that these ethnic Albanians had no real historic ties to Slavic Macedonians and only tenuous political links to the Macedonian state.[5] Based solely on birth projection differences between the Slavic population and ethnic Albanians in Macedonia, it is quite possible that—just as happened between ethnic Albanians and Serbs in Kosovo—Albanians could, at some foreseeable time in the future, become the majority in Macedonia.

In northwest Macedonia, in the regions of Tetovo and Gostivar, the ethnic Albanian population clusters into various *opštine* (communes) that are efficient, well maintained, and help give these Albanian communities a level of prosperity far higher than their kinsmen enjoy elsewhere in the Balkans. Tetovo, for example, became the first community in Macedonia to introduce the Western-style concept of recycling plastic, glass, and tin. These ethnic Albanian communities form a key to the prosperity as well as the viability of the future Macedonia. Indeed, Arben Xhaferi, then leader of the Democratic Party of the Albanians (DPA) had on more than one occasion stated bluntly that *he* was the key to Macedonia's stability.

These regions demanded their share of attention and right to distinct cultural tradition. In 1994, Macedonian authorities bulldozed the so-called "University of Tetovo," which provided instruction in Albanian rather than in the Macedonian language. In 1999, as many as 6,000 students and 300 faculty were conducting classes in cement apartment clusters in a program that remained without accreditation from the government of Macedonia.

In 1998, the mayor of Tetovo, Alajdin Demiri, began serving a prison sentence for raising an Albanian flag outside the city hall. Although later released as a goodwill gesture by the newly elected prime minister of Macedonia, the symbolism of Demiri's gesture could not be ignored. The implications of this seemingly minor event bore significance. (In Kosovo, for example, the symbolism and the irony of the Albanian flag flying over the roofs of ethnic Albanian homes, despite the truth that such homes were located in the Republic of Yugoslavia and not Albania, was not lost on either observers or residents.)[6] With some justification, Albanians regularly complained that they were the victims of systematic discrimination in Macedonia, receiving the worst health care and education and having the least chance for employment in the public sector.

Although American diplomacy regularly cautioned against ethnic Albanians—whether in Albania proper, Kosovo, or Macedonia—officially declaring support or sympathy for the notion of a "Greater Albania," the possibilities of independence and alliance with Albania or Kosovo seemed tempting for Albanians of Macedonia. Thus, Xhaferi's statement that he held the key to stability was not simple hyperbole; it was deadly accurate.

The certainty that a movement toward independence and alliance with Albania would lead to another Balkan war (just as the idea of a "Greater Serbia" led to a Balkan war) remained unclear, however. In retrospect, though, it seemed pertinent to recall that the 1878 "national renaissance"—the *Rilindje kombëtare*—of Albanian history and the idea of a Greater Albania began in Prizren in the Kosovo-Methojia region of Serbia.[7]

Bulgaria

Despite hovering near the abyss of economic collapse ever since 1989, Bulgaria remained the most progressively democratic nation in the Balkans. In hindsight, Daniel Nelson's 1993 suggestion that Bulgaria "would not shrink" from participating in the mayhem and ethnic cleansing that would occur should war break out in the region seems today to have been a somewhat distant possibility.[8] To the contrary, Bulgaria actively sought integration with the West, and desired both NATO and European Union (EU) membership—and eventually joined NATO in 2004.

In actions that Balkan observers tend frequently to ignore, both Bulgaria and Romania—clearly desirous of greater union with the West while unwilling to break their own cultural traditions in the East—cooperated with western Europe on frequent occasions during the 1990s. In 1999, for example, both Romania and Bulgaria offered airspace and territory (as did Macedonia) for NATO and risked retribution from Serbia during the Kosovo intervention. As one result, even as both nations knew that NATO and EU membership were then distant realities, ethnic tensions within their own borders and tense relations with Balkan neighbors had been much reduced.

While it is true that the Second Balkan War of 1913 was fought (and lost) by Bulgaria over Macedonia, it was not a direct correlate that a future Balkan war would be fought for the dismemberment of

Macedonia and the fulfillment of irredentist Bulgarian land claims. (Contemporary Bulgaria, though clearly hobbled by corruption, has a strong parliamentary system that seeks improved rather than deteriorating foreign relations.) Bulgaria was the first nation-state to recognize Macedonia's independence in 1991; of significance, however, was the truth that Bulgaria recognized Macedonia as a state and not as a nation, thus leaving open the door for possible future unification.[9]

Bulgaria and Macedonia have a long and sometimes mutually torturous history. Both were part of the same medieval kingdom, although the cultures and identities of both nations have evolved quite differently over a course of history that has run much longer than the post-1945 Yugoslavia of Marshal Tito. Even the Macedonian language, regarded with open condescension by many Bulgarians as being little more than a dialectical variant, has an alphabet, grammatical morphology, and character distinct from Bulgarian.

Goce Delchev, one of the 1893 founders of the Internal Macedonian Revolutionary Organization *(Vnatreshna Makedonska Revolutsionna Organizatsiya)*, is a symbol of liberation from Ottoman Turks for *both* Bulgaria and Macedonia.[10] (In a failed effort to placate Tito, Josef Stalin pressured Bulgarian Communists in 1947 to relinquish Delchev's bones and allow him to be reburied in the courtyard of the Orthodox Church of Sveti Spas in Skopje, Macedonia.)[11] A number of Bulgarians, most especially those outside the political mainstream, would consider this as one of many examples that suggest that Macedonia is not a separate state but merely an extension of western Bulgaria. Some would cite as evidence how Bulgarian leaders in the nineteenth century purportedly moved their capital to Sofia in the western half of the country to be at the heart of a political and geographical center of a greater Bulgaria.[12] Even today, some voice the sentiment that Macedonia separates itself from Bulgaria only by an artificial frontier and an ersatz dialect of the same language.

Further confusing the issue of identity between the two states is the issue of the so-called "Pirin" Macedonia, a district of Ottoman Macedonia allotted to Bulgaria after the Second Balkan War of 1913. According to some estimates, unofficial census results in 1946 placed the number of ethnic Macedonians in the "Pirin"—which is roughly the region of western Bulgaria that aligns with Macedonia's eastern borders—at 70 percent of the local population.[13] Even in the early 1990s, radical movements within Bulgaria, such as the "Ilinden" Macedonian nationalist organization, seemed proof enough, for some, that Ilinden's goal was to strip away "Pirin" Macedonia from Bulgaria and to incorporate that territory into an independent Macedonia.[14] Yet such movements, which place distinctions on regions in Bulgaria and Macedonia as being either "Vardar" or "Pirin" Macedonia, or identify Greek Macedonia as "Aegean" Macedonia and part of a distinct region that should be reunited, have been marginal, and their influence was largely exaggerated in the political rhetoric of various Balkan nations in the 1990s.

Greece

Greece's sustained objections to Macedonia's original flag, original constitution (which, Greece claimed, established irredentist claims in Greek Macedonia), and use of the name Republic of Macedonia were strenuous throughout the 1990s. Equally, Greece's devastating unilateral trade embargo against Macedonia that lasted until the successful negotiation of the Dayton Accords in 1995 forced Macedonia to rely on sanctions busting, illegal smuggling, and allowed the rise of corrupt criminal networks that continued long after the signing of Dayton. Macedonia learned, in other words, how to live under the mantle of regional conflict and had difficulty adjusting to the legalities of peace.

While much emphasis has been made of the influence of the Greek lobby in the United States,[15] little enough clarity has allowed either the Macedonian or Greek government to realize that far more could be gained through cooperation rather than through asperity. Just as the logic of a Macedonian-Albanian alliance makes reasonable sense, so too does a linking of common Greek-Macedonian interests. Until 1996, no meaningful efforts to establish commercial ties were attempted nonetheless, largely due to the Greek embargo.

The Greek government further denied the presence of a Macedonian minority in northern Greece. Despite the existence of a Macedonian Movement for Balkan Prosperity (*Makedonskí Kínisi Valkanikís Evimerías* or MAKIVE), which published a newspaper titled *Zora* (Dawn) in both Greek and Macedonian, the government only officially recognized the Muslim minority of northern Greece

(referred to in the 1923 Treaty of Lausanne) and refused to acknowledge the existence of any other minority. While some extremist elements, most especially the extremist newspaper *Stóhos* (which literally
means "The Target") called for the "liquidation of all Macedonians,
whether in Greece or elsewhere." Amicable relations between Greeks
(particularly left-wing sympathizers) and Slavic Macedonians in
northern Greece often take place, nonetheless.[16] Individual supporters, such as Christos Sideropoulos and Anastasios Boulis, were
imprisoned, for example, for expressing the belief in media interviews that Slavic Macedonians in Greece were part of a national
ethnic minority.[17]

Exactly how many Slavs in the so-called "Aegean Macedonia" of
northern Greece exist today remains unknown, although estimates
have varied between 10,000 and 300,000.[18] Reality suggests that it
will be highly unlikely in any near foreseeable future that Greece will
recognize the minority of Slavic Macedonians in northern Greece. The
equally evident irony is that Macedonia itself had an opportunity to
establish precedent within its *own* borders by not only recognizing the
validity but also the necessity of ethnic Albanians to receive higher
education in their native language.[19] In a move that would prove contrary to much of recent Balkan history that embraces an "us versus
you" philosophy, Macedonia had the opportunity to gain power by
relinquishing authority. Recognition of the Albanian university in
Tetovo would have *seemed* a requisite first step. (Today, after a decade
of controversy, the Albanian University in Tetovo is legalized.)[20]

Serbia

Serbia, rather than Greece, may well have been Macedonia's
most problematic neighbor from 1991 to 1995. While a senior Greek
diplomat confessed to one of the authors in 1993 that he harbored
the "hope" that Greece and Serbia might eventually and mutually
carve up the tiny republic of Macedonia, his statement was not as
astounding or as confidential as it might first appear. Open source
information reports that Slobodan Milošević, during a 1992 meeting
with Greek Prime Minister Constantine Mitsotakis, openly proposed
that Greece and Serbia partition Macedonia. Moreover, extreme
political leaders in Serbia had stated a desire to share a border with
Greece, which meant the elimination of Macedonia.

Such tensions have a long history. In 1925, for example, the Greek military dictatorship of Theodoros Pangalos declared that Slavic Macedonians were not Macedonians but ethnic Serbs.[21] Although the subsequent Greek government abolished this declaration, it seems worthy to note that in 1999 the foreign minister of Greece, Theodoros Pangalos, was the grandson of the same military dictator.[22]

The Federal Republic of Yugoslavia did not recognize the independence of Macedonia until 1996 and considered the borders between the two states to be merely administrative. Even today, the borders themselves are porous, and a number of points are in contention. Serbia also laid claim to territory along the Macedonian-Serbian border, and there were at least ten points of dispute between the two nations as to what constituted Macedonian or Serbian territory. (It was under this logic that Serbia claimed that it had captured American peacekeepers *within* Serbian territory after NATO's declaration of war against Yugoslavia in March 1999, even as NATO insisted that the soldiers were inside Macedonian territory.)

Even prior to the first two Balkan wars of 1912–1913, both of which were fought in some measure for control of Macedonia, many within Serbia merely considered the territory and the Slavic Macedonians of the region to be part of south Serbia. The largest element of the Serbian minority today lives north of the capital Skopje, in the foothills of Skopska Crna Gora mountain range.[23] Serbia also reportedly armed the small (less than 3 percent) Serbian population within Macedonia and almost unquestionably influenced the stoning of the American Embassy in Skopje on 25 March 1999 by thousands of sympathizers who protested NATO's attacks against Yugoslavia.[24]

When the Yugoslav socialist federation died in 1991, Serbian forces withdrew from Macedonia and confiscated all former Yugoslav weaponry and military equipment, as well as economic and financial assets in the former republic. Macedonia was left without a military and had to start from zero. In some respects, however, the conflicts in Bosnia and in Kosovo left Macedonia with a NATO military protection force and internal security guarantees that it could not have provided for itself in 1999.

Macedonia proved unable to cope with the massive refugee influx that saw hundreds of thousands of ethnic Albanian Kosovars pour into camps in western Macedonia from March to June 1999 and secured the reputation in Western media as being both anti-Albanian and pro-Serb. Neither accusation was entirely accurate. To the contrary, fledgling prime minister Ljupčo Georgievski stated repeatedly that the refugee crisis in Macedonia was similar to 20 million Mexicans crossing into the United States every day even as he accused Yugoslav President Milošević of intentionally driving Kosovar Albanians across the border in order to upset Macedonia's fragile ethnic and religious mix.[25]

If such efforts at destabilization were even partially true, they came perilously close to achieving success during the Kosovo crisis of 1999. A lingering effect was the negative impression Macedonia left in the international community of a nation that was intolerant, incapable, and unwilling to accept the needs of others. In truth, Macedonia had done its best to accommodate Kosovar Albanians and yet it seemed apparent that Macedonia's "best" simply wasn't good enough. Despite the Albanian tradition of *konak*—or hospitality—in which as many as ten Kosovars would sleep in one room of a Macedonian family home, Macedonia was left with an immense refugee problem that left Kosovars with almost no place to go. Both local homes and overcrowded refugee camps could not contain the flood; at one point, a group of fifty Kosovar refugees became so fed up they went to Serbia.[26] In a move partly out of frustration and in what came to be a public relations disaster, the Macedonian government intentionally closed the border between Kosovo and Macedonia in order to goad the West into action.[27] The move, inevitably, backfired.

If Serbia's strategy had been to "destabilize" Macedonia, the effort appeared successful. As a direct result of the Kosovo crisis, tensions between ethnic Albanians and Slavic Macedonians soared; forfeited trade and economic deals for Macedonia exceeded $1.5 billion; and guarantees by President Clinton to secure "the path of prosperity, and even stronger democracy and freedom" were initially and perhaps intentionally ambiguous even as NATO troops used Macedonia as a transit route north for its peacekeeping operations in Kosovo.[28]

Tensions between neighbors in the Balkans have a history that precedes the Cold War by centuries. Both Macedonians and Greeks have, for example, recounted for one of the authors alternate versions of how the medieval kingdom of Bulgaria/Macedonia met its ultimate downfall. After a series of successes against the Byzantine Empire, Czar Samuil's forces met defeat on the slopes of the Belasica mountains at Vodoča: "the place where the eyes were taken out." Byzantine Emperor Basil II, known today as "Basil, the Bulgar Slayer," blinded all but every tenth man of Samuil's 14,000 soldiers. The sighted foot soldiers then led their defeated comrades back to Samuil's palace in Ohrid. According to legend, Czar Samuil, horrified by what he saw, fell dead immediately upon witnessing the return of his defeated army. On the occasions when we heard this episode recounted, we would be reminded of its significance in modern terms, even though this incident took place in the year A.D. 1014.

POST-DAYTON AND POST-KOSOVO REALITIES: 1996–1999

Among the significant challenges Macedonia faces in the future (see Appendices A and B) are the need to improve regional relations and to overcome mutual misperceptions that existed prior to 1995. The belief, for example, that Slobodan Milošević allowed the Yugoslav National Army (JNA) to withdraw in 1992 only to avoid creating a second front during the war in Bosnia-Herzegovina yet fully intended to return to Macedonia in the expectation of the collapse of independence never came to the test.[29] Even if true that the largest part of the Yugoslav army was stationed in south Serbia and Kosovo, and that Serbia did not officially recognize Macedonia until 1996 and currently still disputes some border demarcations, Gligorov asserts in the accompanying interview that a successful withdrawal of Yugoslav forces had been accomplished in a manner that was meant to be permanent.

Further, during interviews conducted in late 1999 with senior foreign service officers who had been stationed in the region during the Kosovo "crisis," Serbia may well be the least of Macedonia's current problems. Indeed, after five years of United Nations Preventive Deployment Forces (UNPREDEP) and subsequent open-ended NATO presence in the region, Milošević, even if he wished to, would simply have been unable to reenter Macedonia unopposed.[30] The issue of the border dispute seemed, in reality, to be little more than a bargaining ploy; Milošević knew that Macedonia's economy could never fully recover as long as Serbia was treated as an international pariah and that Macedonia would never feel fully "secure" as long as its relations—economic and political—with Serbia remained unresolved.

Equally, Albania's support for NATO operations in Kosovo mitigated the nationalist desire to push for the establishment of a Greater Albania. Because Albania had become little more than a chaotic failed state since April 1997, Albania desperately needed European infrastructure and economic support. As a result, no matter how strong the nationalist sentiment among ethnic Albanians for a unified, ethnically homogenous nation, European (and American) discouragement pushed back nationalist sentiment in favor of pragmatic need. Even in Bulgaria, where the most emotional issue was that of a separate "Macedonian" nationality, Bulgaria strove, by fits and starts, to enter Europe. Nationalism, most Bulgarians realized, would not prove in their favor in the long run. That said, in 1999 the opposition party in Bulgaria was both anti-NATO and anti-Western; fortunes and policies could change more quickly than most analysts believed possible. Bulgaria seemed most comfortable establishing a relationship with Macedonia based on dominance rather than parity.

Finally, among Greeks—the most pragmatic and prosperous of all Balkan peoples—there was an incentive that appeared to be compelling: economic profit. Despite Greece's intransigence on the issue of the name *Macedonia,* Greek businesses rapidly established commercial relations; in some ways, Greece secured Macedonia as an economic protectorate. Employing its Balkan prominence as EU and NATO member to establish business and trade with its neighbor to the north, for Greece the prospect of doing business in a stable Macedonia seemed too tempting to resist. In retrospect, apparent Greek (and Serbian) irredentist claims against Macedonia only a few years previous had effectively been muted by other realities.

None of these relations, it should be stressed, were set in permanent alignment at the end of the twentieth century. Relationships could easily destabilize, and new governments in the region could intentionally craft alternative policies toward their neighbors. In 1999, however, despite or perhaps because of the horrors that had taken place in Bosnia-Herzegovina and in Kosovo, Macedonia appeared to be making progress—painful and slow—in the right direction. In August 1999, for example, Macedonian Prime Minister Ljupčo Georgievski and Greek minister Costas Simitis met in the village of Flórina (known in Macedonia as Lerin) during a cultural exchange program. Although nothing immediately substantive came from the meeting, the leaders of these two nations exchanged perspectives and offered each other praise in a series of cordial discussions. This meeting seemed virtually unthinkable only a few years previous. In August 1995, Greece had imposed a unilateral trade embargo against Macedonia; in August 1999, Greece and Macedonia were looking for ways to increase economic prosperity.

INTERNAL POLITICS: COALITIONS, COMPROMISE, CONDITIONS

The Macedonian domestic political scene has had its own set of unique circumstances during the last decade of the twentieth century.[31] Although President Kiro Gligorov handily won reelection to the Macedonian presidency and served throughout his term of office (including after surviving an assassination attempt in October 1995), the major political parties witnessed complete reversals of fortune. The Social Democratic Alliance of Macedonia (SDSM) won parliamentary elections in 1992 and 1994 as the ruling party of the two coalitions that governed after independence. In opposition, the Internal Macedonian Revolutionary Organization (IMRO), which took its name from the terrorist organization of the late nineteenth century, had established a hard-line, nationalist agenda and had become a kind of *Sinn Féin* without an Irish Republican Army behind it.[32] In 1994, after failing to repeat its earlier successes in the first round of parliamentary elections, IMRO boycotted the second round and appeared to have permanently marginalized itself from power and political influence in Macedonia.

By 1998, however, the situation had changed. Equally, the belief expressed by some observers that IMRO had permanently acceded power and influence in Macedonian politics was not true. In November 1998, IMRO replaced the SDSM as the majority party and formed what appeared to be an unusual coalition with the Albanian Democratic Party of Arben Xhaferi. Vasil Tupurkovski's newly formed Democratic Alternative Party, as well as a fourth political party that called itself the Liberal Democratic Party (LDP), completed the ruling coalition that suffered through the stress of regional war and the massive refugee influx into Macedonia of Kosovars in 1999.[33]

LJUPČO GEORGIEVSKI AND IMRO

It seems paradoxical that the leader of the Internal Macedonian Revolutionary Organization and Macedonia's newly elected prime minister would secure a reputation during the Kosovar crisis of 1999 as being unwilling to support aid efforts to stem the Kosovo crisis and reluctant to provide all but the most minimal assistance to the massive number of refugees. The truth and the irony of that truth are quite different. Georgievski not only worked to provide assistance; he allowed 12,000 NATO troops to deploy along the Kosovo border without, initially, having any guarantees of Macedonia's internal security should the nation have been brought into a wider conflict.

Georgievski, an avowed anti-Communist and advocate of Macedonian independence since the 1980s, modified his nationalist stance in the 1990s and became a professed advocate of ethnic tolerance and moderation, even serving to check the more extreme nationalist members of his governing coalition. The most obvious example of this moderation came when Georgievski sought to integrate rather than marginalize Xhaferi's Albanian party as a member of the government coalition in 1998. Slavs and Albanians, long depicted as bitter enemies, now depended on each other for Macedonia's internal stability.

Born in 1966, and leader of IMRO since 1990, Georgievski was the youngest political leader in Macedonia's brief history. Although appointed vice president in the first democratically elected government in 1991, he almost immediately resigned in order to become leader of the political opposition. Failing to repeat his parliamentary election success in 1994, he withdrew from the second round and, with the aid of other political parties, helped organize so-called "parallel" elections that were not recognized by the Organization for Security and Cooperation in Europe (OSCE).

By 1999, though matured, Georgievski's political skills were sorely tested, and he accused Yugoslav President Milošević directly of trying to destroy Macedonia. Referring to the expulsion of

Kosovar refugees, the prime minister claimed that "Milošević plays on the fact of the Christian-Muslim conflict. . . . He plays to the fears of the Christians that a surplus of Muslim refugees will make Muslims predominant."[34] Since only 40,000 Serbs live in Macedonia (fewer than the number of Macedonian Gypsies), an insurgent ethnic uprising by Serbs, similar to what happened to Croatia in 1991, seemed unlikely. Whether by political acumen or chance—or total dominance of his party—Georgievski managed to survive the storm, however temporarily. One central goal of his government's policy, nonetheless, had little chance in the near term: Macedonia's acceptance into NATO membership.

ARBEN XHAFERI AND THE DPA

Depending on which claim is presented, Macedonia's ethnic Albanian population prior to March 1999 formed anywhere between 20 to 40 percent of the total population.[35] (Although outdated, 1994 census figures place this number at less than a quarter.) Political leader Arben Xhaferi was correct in his assertion that only 3 percent of this Albanian population was employed in the public sector, armed forces, courts, media, and cultural organizations. Intriguingly, Xhaferi seemed a pragmatist rather than a fundamentalist.[36] "We have two problems. The effort to marginalize Albanians in the society is one. The more inherent problem is the Islamization of Albanian culture."[37]

Neither an advocate for a religious state nor a separatist, Xhaferi most commonly learned the best lesson of Balkan politics: to keep one's head down in order to survive and learn how to get along with a potential enemy. Toward that end, he agreed to form part of IMRO's governing coalition in 1998, declaring that "We can find common ground for ethnic integration through mutual understanding."[38] Such admirable declarations have not always been consistent ones. Xhaferi, recognizing how pivotal his influence had become, had previously threatened the secession of ethnic Albanians from the Macedonian state and a possible alignment with a Greater Albania. Both Xhaferi's DPA and the largely ethnic Albanian and Turkish Party for Democratic Prosperity (PDP) pushed the Macedonian government in 1999 to recognize the Kosovo Liberation Army—*Ushtria*

Çlirimtare e Kosovës—known also as the UÇK, the national army of independent Kosovo.

Xhaferi's DPA party stemmed from what was considered the "radical" wing of the PDP that seceded in 1994.[39] He openly advocated turning the Macedonian state into a federation. Indeed, both Georgievski's and Xhaferi's past actions and statements, prior to joining the 1998 Macedonian coalition, stood in stark contrast to their more moderate stances once centered in a position of power.

VASIL TUPURKOVSKI AND THE DEMOCRATIC ALTERNATIVE

Tupurkovski, who formed his alliance shortly before the 1998 elections, was one of the most seasoned politicians in Macedonia. A professor of international law and member of the law faculty at Cyril and Methodios University in Skopje, he formed the Democratic Alternative—or *Demokratska Alterniva*—just prior to the 1998 elections. His party held eight ministerial posts and the speaker of parliament position as well as seats for sixteen parliament members. In 1991, as the Macedonian representative and one of eight voting members of the bizarre Yugoslav Federal Presidency instituted after Tito's death, Tupurkovski fought, in vain, to prevent the dissolution of the Yugoslav state.[40] His long-term expectation, both for the survival of Macedonia and for the recovery of the Balkan region, is that Western governments and businesses must provide economic aid, infrastructure support, and direct investment.

During the time when Yugoslavia still existed, Tupurkovski was a popular figure, both within Macedonia and within the ailing nation-state. Physically huge and affable, he was commonly known as *Džemperovski* ("Sweater-man") because of his preference for casual clothes and inclination to take public transport rather than the various foreign import cars preferred by other Yugoslav politicians.[41] Following the death of the Yugoslav nation, Tupurkovski resurfaced to provide a form of influence, albeit small, on the evolving Macedonian political identity. His own commentary on the political reality that both Georgievski's IMRO and Xhaferi's DPA faced was revealing: "They [IMRO and DPA] realized perfectly well they could never have won with the radical positions they used to hold, and they really wanted to win, and to hold power."[42]

CONCLUSION: MOVING BEYOND HOPE AND AMBIGUITY

In the Balkans, all the other countries are a problem. We, Macedonia, want to be the stable country.
                    —*Vasil Tupurkovski, 1998*

Macedonia, during the 1990s, came perilously close to internal collapse on more than one occasion. Aside from a failure to complete secure resolution with Greece over various disputes, its internal commitments to economic reform were never fully committed to during the 1990s. Further, geographical isolation, obvious lack of technological sophistication as well as lack of access to technology, and evident and continuing political instability—severely aggravated by the Kosovo crisis of 1999—failed to encourage foreign investment over the long run. That said, such investment along with the successful implementation of economic reforms were the only means to secure stability or ensure Macedonia's long-term success.

If one were to take a retrospective look at the Balkans in general over the last decade of the twentieth century, it might indeed seem miraculous that Macedonia had not suffered a fate similar to that of its neighbors. The future for Macedonia seemed laced with promise as much as peril. One evident conclusion is that the tensions between Slavic Macedonians and ethnic Albanians would continue at some aggravated level of contest. The solution, nonetheless, could only be achieved by the peoples of the region. Such evidence should have become a viable marker for other troubled nations of the region.

A further and far more troubling conclusion centered on the obvious neglect Macedonia received from the West during the years of its early independence. Treated largely as a staging area for NATO operations both prior to, during, and after the Kosovo engagement of 1999, it remained unclear how firm the West's security, economic, and even political commitments to Macedonia's future success were. Such ambiguity, while providing the West with a means to escape culpability, also invoked an inevitable bitterness in the Macedonians themselves. Sašo Ordanoski, editor of the Macedonian *Forum* magazine and normally an optimistic Balkan observer, remarked grimly in 1999 that Macedonia was forced to end up paying the bill for Serbia's injustice against Kosovo's Albanians. In the end, he added, if NATO countries had used only a small proportion of what they had spent on bombs to modernize Macedonia and other Balkan countries, the region would have had a far better chance not only for integration but for survival.[43]

Today Macedonia is the last genuinely multiethnic state in the Balkans. For some, this suggests the impossibility of its continued existence. Cynics, often with no Balkan experience or knowledge, can be quite brutal in their ideas and so-called resolutions. John Mearsheimer and Stephen Van Evera, for instance, suggested that:

> If the Slavs refuse to share more equally with the Albanians, violence is inevitable. To forestall this, NATO should consider calling for a plebiscite to determine whether the Albanians want to remain in Macedonia. If not, Macedonia should also be partitioned. This is feasible because the Albanians of Macedonia are concentrated in western Macedonia, next to Kosovo and Albania.[44]

Such a "solution" is flawed by internal contradictions. Why NATO should have violated its own standard of avowed postconflict neutrality and take on the role of mandating plebiscites, normally the role of institutions such as the OSCE, was unclear. Why Albanians of western Macedonia, Kosovo, and Albania itself should be aligned with (read, "partitioned") a community that would represent the poorest ethnic entity in Europe, and yet be separated—physically, psychologically, economically—from the very ethnic communities and trading blocs they would depend on (such as the "Slavs" of Macedonia) and be somehow expected to remain viable is doubtful. Why Mearsheimer and Van Evera could not recognize that the partition they advocated as yet another barbaric form of ethnic cleansing, and more than just an "ugly formula for ending wars," is astounding.

In retrospect, it seems odd to realize how little credit or acknowledgment Macedonia has received for its success since independence. As Arben Xhaferi once expressed it, this success is compelled by the inevitable allure of the West. "Spiritually," he claimed, ethnic

Albanians "are with the East, but their self-interest lies in the West."[45] Equally ironic is the truth that when the European Union established a five-member Arbitration Commission in November 1991, chaired by Judge Robert Badinter of France, to determine the recognition status of Yugoslav republics, four former Yugoslav republics applied: Slovenia, Croatia, Bosnia-Herzegovina, and Macedonia. The Badinter Commission, as it came to be known, evaluated each applicant on the basis of how each republic seeking independence would provide adequate protection for minorities as well as control of its own frontiers. The commission released its results on 15 January 1992, indicating that only two former republics sufficiently met the established criteria for recognition by the European Community: Slovenia and Macedonia.

Slovenia, a largely ethnically homogenous nation with an individual per capita income that rivals that of Greece, was destined to join the ranks of both the European Union and NATO in 2004. Macedonia, by contrast, remained an ethnically diverse nation and the poorest of the former Yugoslav republics.

No matter how difficult the choices for the people and for the region, it is no accident that the Macedonian question of the nineteenth century was resurrected in a new form in the late-twentieth century. Yet this new Macedonian "question"—one that focuses on identity—required a frank assessment of that nation's necessity and probability for survival. Perhaps the most complete irony is that Macedonia's fate could have been determined, and may well yet be, by specific and strategic policy choices rather than by a fatalistic coin toss left to the indiscriminate and often brutal gods of chance.

NOTES

1. Yugoslavia is known today simply as Serbia and Montenegro.

2. Extracted from private correspondence with the writer Bogomil Gjuzel, 1996.

3. Carol J. Williams, "Macedonia Sees Highway as Its Route to Recovery," *Los Angeles Times,* July 6, 1993, 5.

4. Micahel G. Roskin, "Macedonia and Albania: The Missing Alliance," *Parameters* (Winter 1993–94): 91–92; 93–94.

5. Marshall Freeman Harris, "Macedonia: The Next Domino?" *National Interest* (Spring 1999): 42–43.

6. Indeed, in 2004, ethnic Albanians pushed to pass legislation allowing the Albanian flag to fly outside Macedonia's parliament, claiming the flag itself symbolized the Albanian "nation."

7. Noel Malcolm, *Kosovo: A Short History* (New York: New York University Press, 1998), 217; 222–23.

8. Daniel Nelson, "A Balkan Perspective," *Strategic Review* (Winter 1993): 29.

9. Roskin, "Macedonia and Albania," 96.

10. To complicate matters further, Delchev was actually born in northern Greece in the village known variously as Kukuš (in Macedonian) or Kilkis (in Greek).

11. Robert D. Kaplan, *Balkan Ghosts: A Journey through History* (New York: St. Martin's Press, 1993), 59.

12. Harris, "Macedonia," 43.

13. Valentina Georgieva and Sasha Konechni, *Historical Dictionary of the Republic of Macedonia* (Lanham, MD: Scarecrow Press, 1998), 191.

14. Ilinden derives from the national day of Macedonia: St. Elijah's Day. On that day, 4 August 1903, Macedonian rebels declared an independent republic in the region of modern Macedonia named Kruševo. The Republic of Kruševo lasted until August 12, 1903, when the Ottoman army surrounded the rebel forces and massacred most of the town's inhabitants.

15. Harris "Macedonia," 1999, 44–45.

16. Peter Hill, "Macedonians in Greece and Albania: A Comparative Study of Recent Developments," *Nationalities Papers* 27, no. 1 (1999): 20.

17. While living and working in Greece from 1993 to 1996, P. H. Liotta heard Hellenic colleagues refer to Sideropoulos on several occasions as a *jenitsaros* or "janizary," implying that he had been brainwashed and was committing a form of treachery. On numerous occasions, while traveling in northern Greece, particularly in the area of Flórina/Lerin and in the Prespa Lakes region, he heard the Macedonian language spoken on a regular basis. (Equally, he often saw graffiti written in Greek on village walls that read: "Northern Epiros [that is, southern Albania] is now and forever Greek.")

18. Human Rights Watch/Helsinki Watch, *Denying Ethnic Identity: The Macedonians of Greece* (New York: Human Rights Watch, 1994), 12–13.

19. Albanians *do* receive education in their native language at both the primary and secondary levels.

20. Today this is a non-issue in Macedonia, although real tensions exist between interethnic Slav and Albanian communists over public education. The official Macedonian position was that it was not feasible to support a program exclusively in the Albanian language at one university. (Indeed, a number have suggested that graduate studies would probably serve students best if held in English, since only a limited number of people speak either

Macedonian or Albanian and English has increasingly become the language of globalization.) Further, instruction in Albanian already occurs at the Cyril and Methodios University. Until Kosovo was stripped of its autonomy in 1989, there was an agreement between Macedonia and Kosovo to provide education in Albanian at the University of Priština, and an exchange program still exists that allows ethnic Albanians from Macedonia to study at the University of Tiranë in Albania.

21. Georgieva and Konechni, *Historical Dictionary*, 1998, 180.

22. Greek minister Costas Simitis dismissed Pangalos from his foreign ministry position in February 1999, for the complicity that Greek officials had had with the Kurdish separatist, Abdullah Öcalan, prior to Turkish armed forces seizing him at the airport in Nairobi, Kenya, as well as for the failure of Greek authorities to prevent Öcalan's seizure. Georgios Papandreou, son of the former prime minister, assumed Pangalos's position as foreign minister.

23. Georgieva and Konechni, *Historical Dictionary*, 1998, 221.

24. Alessandra Stanley, "In Macedonia: Embassies Are Stoned as Tensions Begin to Rise,"*New York Times,* March 26, 1999, A10.

25. Carlotta Gall, "In Macedonia: Yugoslav Neighbor Fears an Effort to 'Destabilize' It," *New York Times,* April 15, 1999, A12.

26. Jonathan Alter and Carla Power, "The Next Balkan Domino?" *Newsweek,* May 31, 1999, 39.

27. Carlotta Gall, "In Macedonia: Many Fear Where They're Going, as Well as Where They've Been," *New York Times,* April 7, 1999, A11.

28. John Tagliabue, "The World: Alive and Ailing in the Balkans," *New York Times,* Week in Review, June 27, 1999, 3.

29. Georgieva and Konechni, *Historical Dictionary*, 1998, 85.

30. In 1999 few people outside Macedonia recognized that the real threat to state security would come from within, as it did in 2001.

31. Perhaps indicative of vibrant pluralism as well as chaos, there are over sixty officially registered political parties in Macedonia. For a nation of slightly more than two million, this seems extraordinary. Macedonia can also take credit in being the only nation in the world to have first popularly elected a Roma, or Gypsy, member of parliament.

32. IMRO's actual title is VMRO-Democratic Party for National Unity, from the Macedonian *Vnatreshna Makedonska Revolutsionna Organizatsiya,* and is one of a number of political parties to have appropriated the VMRO designation for its identity. (VMRO-Fatherland, VMRO-United, and the VMRO-Goce Delchev-Radical Democratic Party are three other examples.) All such organizations claim that their existence is a continuation of the original Macedonian Revolutionary Organization created in 1893 and based in Thessaloniki, Greece. For simplicity, the term IMRO is used here rather than the more bulky yet correct marker of VMRO/DPMNE or IMRO/DPMNU.

33. The smallest member of the coalition, the LDP, held only one ministerial post, and only four of its members served in parliament. In August 1999, following the accidental death of the LDP minister "without portfolio" following a highway collision with a NATO K-FOR vehicle, the LDP withdrew from the coalition.

34. Gall, "In Macedonia," A12.

35. 1994 census figures claim Slavic Macedonians as the largest ethnic group, with 66.5 percent, or 1,288,330, of the total population of 1,936,877 inhabitants. Ethnic Albanians comprise 22.9 percent, 442,914. Ethnic Turks comprise 4 percent; ethnic Serbs, 2 percent, and ethnic Roma (Gypsies) account for 43,762, or 2.3 percent (Georgieva and Konechni, *Historical Dictionary,* 1998, 195–196).

36. Again for the sake of simplicity in what can only be termed a convoluted process, Xhaferi's party is referred to here as the DPA (the Democratic Party of the Albanians), despite the fact that party rulership and legal complications prevent its official registration with this designation; instead, Xhaferi's party was actually the PDP-A (Party for the Democratic Prosperity of Albanians) and in 1999 held eight ministerial posts with eleven members of parliament.

37. Alessandra Stanley, "In Macedonia: Balkan Rarity: A Peaceful Mixture of Ethnic Groups, All Looking to the West," *New York Times,* March 29, 1999, A10.

38. Mike O'Connor, "Slavs and Albanians Form Unusual Coalition in Macedonia," *New York Times,* November 30, 1998, A6.

39. Georgiea and Konechni, *Historical Dictionary,* 259.

40. Tupurkovski hails not from Macedonia proper but from Greek Macedonia, which Macedonians commonly refer to as the Aegean part of Macedonia. Given the antagonism between Greece and Macedonia over the proper use of names and regional identities, the term *Aegean* Macedonia can prove problematic.

41. Laura Silber and Allan Little, *Yugoslavia: Death of a Nation* (New York: TV Books, 1996), 125.

42. O'Connor, "Slavs and Albanians Form," A6.

43. "Macedonia and its Kosovars: In the Balance," *Economist,* May 8, 1999, 52.

44. John J. Mearsheimer and Stephen Van Evera, "Redraw the Map, Stop the Killing," *New York Times,* April 19, 1999. http://www.nytimes.com/yr/mo/day/oped/19mear.html

45. Stanley, "In Macedonia," A10.

Spillover Effect:
Aftershocks in Kosovo,
Macedonia, and Serbia

On 24 March 1999, NATO went to war against Yugoslavia. Ten weeks later, President Slobodan Milošević capitulated to the alliance's demands.[1] Thus, the NATO intervention against Yugoslavia, during which the alliance suffered no casualties, may prove to be a pivotal event in European security. Yet much of former Yugoslavia seems to hover in tenuous uncertainty, Kosovo remains an international protectorate, and Macedonia's fate is uncertain. Further, as the chronology of events in the following chapter will illustrate, aftershock events of the post-Kosovo intervention led to security degradation in Macedonia in 2001 and seriously hampered the recovery efforts of Serbia after the "October Revolution" of 2000.

This essay challenges the conventional wisdom that there are definite "lessons" to be drawn from NATO's war over Kosovo. To the contrary, the Kosovo intervention offers a number of compelling (and often contradictory) implications that should concern—and may even confound—serious analysts and policymakers. At best, the most reasonable conclusion, in the aftermath of the war, is that the lessons of Kosovo are terminally ambiguous.

This observation, however, is not without merit. While our intent here is not to promote a specific solution or set of policy recommendations, we do present a broad problem set of dynamics that were and are driving forces in the shaping, analysis, and future direction of the European security architecture. Attempts to explain conflict that focus too narrowly on ethnic differences or too broadly evoke human justice as grounds for intervention will consistently miss the strategic mark.

Listed below are five of the compelling but often contradictory "truths" of the Kosovo intervention:

- The divisions between Serbs and Kosovars will continue long into the future.
- The arguments for humanitarian intervention in Kosovo, while articulate and often reasoned, do not establish a solid precedent for future violations of sovereignty on behalf of human rights.
- If Kosovo is to have any chance of survival, international peacekeeping forces and personnel committed to infrastructure and administrative oversight must remain—probably indefinitely. (This suggestion directly contradicts the focus of the George Bush administration, which wanted "out" of the Balkans specifically, and Europe generally, as fast as possible.)
- Kosovo and "aftermath events" in Macedonia and Serbia underscore the dangerous precedent that ethnic communities that use violence are thereby able to solidify their internal identity and are more likely to obtain external support than those that do not adopt violent methods.
- Despite the bleak implications of the four preceding propositions, the prospects for Kosovo and the southern Balkans are not hopeless.

While doubtless frustrating to the reader searching for specific and predictable explanations, the dynamics listed here will continue, often in mutual conflict, to pressure the region and its people. Essentially, both are caught in a vicious cycle: Serbs resent how Kosovo has prevented Yugoslavia from returning to the European fold yet were reluctant to let go; Kosovo's Albanians longed for independence from Serbia and now saw it as a possibility; the international community (especially the United Nations) oversaw Kosovo as a protectorate but was unwilling to support its too rapid independence from Serbia. Individually and collectively, these dynamics will distress and continue to prevent clear or definable outcomes. Further, while some progress—however slow—has been achieved in Kosovo, there are indeed spillover effects in Macedonia and in Serbia that have direct relations with the aftermath of the 1999 Kosovo intervention.

KOSOVO: A PERFECT FAILURE?

In August 1999, the newly appointed U.S. ambassador to the United Nations, Richard Holbrooke, stood at the edge of a mass grave near the Stara Cikatova quarry in Kosovo. One hundred and twenty-nine bodies had been exhumed from three different sites in the quarry. Investigators claimed that, during the NATO campaign against Yugoslavia, ethnic Albanians had been marched to the edge of a cliff, shot, and then dumped into the quarry, with dead cattle piled on top of them.[2] Holbrooke, who had negotiated the Bosnian Dayton Accords and later broke off negotiations with Milošević over Kosovo in late March 1999, was the diplomat most responsible for American policy in the Balkans and was often regarded by Europeans as a kind of imperial proconsul.[3] He paused slightly at the human spectacle of these graves and the symbol of what had occurred during the war over the region. The ambassador, uncharacteristically, was at a loss for words.

Reality was all too evident that day, for peace between the Serbs and the Kosovar Albanians was far off. Indeed, the systematic execution of fourteen Serb farmers outside Priština in late July was equally horrific.[4] The farmers had been harvesting wheat near their village of Gračko when they were gunned down at close range with automatic weapons.[5] Although the Kosovo Liberation Army denied responsibility for the incident, its meaning was evident: Hearts and minds would continue to be consumed by revenge.

Under the auspices of a larger so-called international community, NATO established an extraordinary postconflict precedent in Kosovo: the permanent occupation of part of a sovereign state. The protectorate was not openly allowed, or encouraged, to seek independence. As 1999 came to a close, the UN administrator for the province, Bernard Kouchner, announced that a condition of supervisional power sharing had been arranged between the Kosovar political leadership and the international community. While not a full declaration of support by the UN for Kosovo's independence, this move posed contradictions nonetheless.

Given the complexity of that dynamic, and the numerous challenges entailed in sorting out the responsibilities and activities of the United Nations Mission in Kosovo (UNMIK) and the Kosovo Force (K-FOR), it seems nothing short of miraculous that there was any form of effective control at all in postconflict Kosovo. By the end of 1999, the peacekeeping troops had, according to some observers, reached the limit of their intervention potential and were simply functioning as a heavily armed policing force.[6] Yet under the subsequent "interim" administration of former Dutch defense minister Hans Haekkerup, UNMIK laid claim to economic, judicial, administrative, and legislative authority in the province. By direct intervention as well, UNMIK tempered the rise of a hard-line "provisional government" in Kosovo that would seek independence from Serbia at the earliest opportunity.

On 15 May 2001, Haekkerup signed into law the Constitutional Framework for Provisional Self-Government. Although clearly not a mandate for Kosovo's independence, the framework—coupled with the elections of 17 November 2001—set the stage on which the agenda for substantial autonomy and self-government in Kosovo could be accomplished.

It seems premature to declare, as some have done, that the war against Yugoslavia was a "military success and political failure."[7] To the contrary, the opposite outcome, though less intuitively obvious perhaps, has proven true. Given the daunting challenges of the situation, what has happened in postconflict Kosovo has a logic and sensibility all its own. Impossible situations, after all, still demand a political "fix" to the military conundrum known as humanitarian war.

Power Shifts

Kosovo's multiethnic assembly, consisting of 120 deputies from across Kosovo, held its inaugural session on 10 December 2001. This was its first convocation in the more than twelve years since Slobodan Milošević had stripped it of its authority and its autonomy from Serbia in 1989.

The message of reconciliation was overshadowed when members of the Democratic Party of Kosovo (PDK), under the leadership of former Kosovo Liberation Army leader Hashim Thaqi, walked out of the assembly hall in protest at their proposals being ignored. Although the assembly, dominated by independence-minded Albanian parties, was meant in principle to establish a body that could democratically determine the means and mechanisms for self-rule, the brief walkout by the PDK, the second-largest political party, showed that power politics—and power struggles—remained very much in play. As background, a brief review of the history and tensions that led to the historic 2001 assembly meeting might prove useful.

THE RISE OF THE KLA

By late 1999, the leadership of the Kosovo Liberation Army (KLA)—known in Albanian as *Ushtria Çlirimtare e Kosovës*—had effectively assumed power in the province as a "provisional government."[8] This organization, referred to only a year before by Robert Gelbard, the Clinton administration's envoy to the region, as a "terrorist organization," had now eliminated Ibrahim Rugova and his Democratic League (LDK) as a viable peaceful alternative. The KLA had set the stage to win Kosovo's long-sought independence. Indeed, it seemed determined to force Kosovo to become, as had almost all the successor states to the former Yugoslavia, yet another of what some derisively considered to be ex-Yugoslavia's "moral and intellectual dwarfs."[9]

The KLA, nevertheless, had learned to accommodate. As head of its political directorate, Thaqi, whose *nom de guerre* was "The Snake," had earned a reputation for executing competitors for leadership of the organization during his infamous rise to power. By June 1999, he had established a rival "provisional" government to Rugova's self-declared "republic" in Kosovo and had established himself as prime minister.[10] Displaying wily political skills that confounded Madeleine Albright during the February 1999 negotiations at Rambouillet, Thaqi found a way around the principles established in France as the basis for a peace agreement between Belgrade and the KLA:

- Withdrawal of military and paramilitary forces from Kosovo
- Restoration of Kosovo's political autonomy
- A three-year transitional period, followed by a referendum on Kosovo's future status

- Disarming of the KLA
- Deployment of an armed NATO peacekeeping force to Yugoslavia[11]

The blame as well as the credit for Kosovo's remarkable break from Yugoslavia should not go entirely to the KLA, however. Rugova's efforts in the early 1990s, for example, clearly laid the groundwork and provided the symbolic means by which Kosovar Albanians could imagine their nominal freedom from oppression and the creation, one day, of a separate Wilsonian state based on the notion of self-determination.[12] Rugova's failure to progress toward the realization of this idea, coupled with the consistent failure of the "West" to shore up his legitimacy, left him in a position in which, at best, he appeared to have done no more than reach an accommodating stalemate with his Serbian overlords in Belgrade.[13]

The KLA, on the other hand, was able to capitalize on the dynamic and secure a tentative, though continuing, compromise with NATO and the K-FOR forces in postconflict Kosovo. Although nominally the KLA was transformed into a much smaller civilian defense corps and turned thousands of weapons over to NATO control, the amount of firepower available to the Kosovars remained significant. As part of the arms windfall that followed the Albanian government's collapse in April 1997, sources indicate anywhere from 650,000 to 750,000 Kalashnikovs and 3 million hand grenades flowed north to Kosovo shortly after the spring of that year, often ending up in the hands of ethnic Albanians who were ungoverned, destitute, and steeped in the medieval Albanian tradition of blood vengeance.[14] Diaspora Albanian communities, particularly in the United States, further facilitated the rise of the KLA by providing funds and munitions that gave Kosovars the violent means to achieve their dreamed-for ends.[15]

The municipal elections of 28 October 2000, in which Rugova's party won 60 percent of the vote, and the province-wide November 2001 elections (Table 1), in which it won the election but did not secure enough votes to establish a majority government, suggest that there is no clear mandate for Kosovo's future—other than an insistence on independence from Serbia. Some voters apparently felt that Rugova was the most palatable choice for the West and, therefore, the best hedge to lead the people of Kosovo down the popular path

TABLE 1 November 2001 Kosovo Assembly Elections.

Party	Description	Percentage of seats	Number of seats (of 120)
Democratic League of Kosovo (LDK)	Dominant political force in Kosovo, led by Ibrahim Rugova. Largely the leader of passive resistance to Serbian rule during the 1990s. Unswervingly supports independence but maintains cooperative stance toward international authorities.	46.3	47
Democratic Party of Kosovo (PDK)	Second-strongest party, led by Hashim Thaqi. Formed in September 1999. Largely seen as successor to Kosovo Liberation Army (KLA). Full support for independence. Most outspoken critic of constitutional framework but willing to work within it.	25.5	26
Kosovo Serb Return Coalition	Party of the Serbian minority.	11.0	22
Alliance for the Future of Kosovo (AAK)	Formed in May 2000 as an alliance of six parties (later reduced to four), this is the youngest of the three main parties, led by Ramush Haradinaj. Also a supporter of independence. Challenges PDK as KLA-successor. Tries to differentiate itself by saying it represents hard work and effective government.	7.8	8

Source: Election result figures taken from ElectionWorld.org

toward self-determination. Caustic observers might even suggest that
the United Nations Mission in Kosovo, through divide-and-rule and
authoritarian tactics, created this democratic mess by permitting new
political parties to register with only fifty signatures.[16] By doing this,
UNMIK prevented the centralized control of the more radical "provisional elements" that were unpalatable to the international community,
and at the same time it was able to resurrect Rugova, whose reputation
had been tarnished by perceived failures in leadership in the 1990s,
especially during the NATO campaign against Milošević in 1999.

UNMIK's actions clearly strengthened Rugova's party, which
by 2001 was both experienced and well funded. Yet, perhaps dis-
turbingly, this external intervention also suggested a potential frac-
tionalization among the Kosovars themselves, in which preferences
for leadership turned more toward kin and community than toward
an overarching single leadership for Kosovo.

THICKER THAN WATER?

In the wake of the collapse of communism and the Albanian government's 1997 structural failure and subsequent implosion, perhaps
not enough attention centered on the reality that Kosovo would not
be able to function as a coherent state should it gain independence.
Moreover, some Kosovars do not want Kosovo to function in such a
manner. One of the overlooked outcomes of the 1990s Balkan chaos
was the return of the kin communities and tribal identities that now
dominate more stylized visions of central authority and governmental control.[17]

The notion of blood feuds between clans, for example, as well
as the decentralized control that drove regional disintegration in the
1990s, helped create a chasm between city and village, and between
individual citizens and a collective identity. Perhaps the most striking
indication of this tendency—true for Muslims and Christians alike—
was the return of the "blood" code, or *kanun* (from the Greek for
"canon"), to rural areas and then to outlying cities. The most infamous
of the many codes is the fifteenth-century *kanun* of the Albanian
nobleman Lekë Dukagjin.

Lekë's code is based on a male-predominant ethic to protect and
uphold family honor. As a medieval form of justice, it was actually

intended to limit bloodshed among feudal factions. As such, the code is said to have had more local authority than the Ten Commandments.[18] Variants of the code specify how a man must avenge his honor through blood for acts that dishonor the code, such as calling him a liar in front of other men, taking his weapons, insulting his wife, or violating the hospitality afforded a guest in his home.

During its oral transmission over the generations, the code underwent numerous local transmutations. Sections of the *kanun* did not appear in print until the nineteenth century, and it was first formally collected and published in its entirety by an Albanian Roman Catholic priest, Father Shtjefën Gjeçov.[19] While the notion of blood revenge was by no means restricted to Albanians in the Balkans (the mass expulsion of Kosovar Albanians by Yugoslav forces during March–June 1999 is a pertinent example), the Albanian codification of blood vengeance pointed to a problem of the post–Cold War era: The Balkan ethic of blood revenge, largely though not completely suppressed after World War I, returned with a vengeance in times of state disintegration and civil war.[20] In effect, the members of extended families became bound to one another rather than to the state.[21]

Although the Albanian communist regime of Enver Hoxha brutally repressed those who practiced the *kanun*, the complete absence of authority fueled its return with a vengeance.[22] Admittedly only a small part of a complex dynamic, the *kanun*'s aversion to controlling forces from outside the clan has made cooperation with NATO and K-FOR a complicated matter. The systematic execution of fourteen Serb farmers in Gračko in July 1999, for example, though not proven to have been an act of blood vengeance, bears numerous echoes of the *kanun*. Chapter 157 of the code, known as the "fire-torch and axe" punishments, is specific against those accused of harming the clan, or of committing ethnic cleansing, for that matter: "If someone commits these crimes, he is executed by the village, his family is fined, his house is burned, his trees are cut down, his gardens and vineyards are destroyed, and his *survivors are expelled from the country with their belongings*"[23] (emphasis added). On a grand scale, it would be difficult to provide a more succinct synopsis of the Kosovo disaster of 1999—or its aftermath.

THE IDEA OF SOVEREIGNTY

Although military engagements and the large-scale humanitarian disaster of Kosovo presented the ugliest reality of Balkan division and ethnic separation, there was also a certain elegance in the forceful determination of the idealists who supported NATO's war against Yugoslavia. UN Secretary-General Kofi Annan, for example, in his September 1999 speech to the General Assembly, focused on the right of individual citizens to protection even at the expense of state sovereignty.

In this 1999 address and again in his speech in 2001 upon receiving the Nobel Peace Prize, Annan upheld the idea that the "common interest" of humanity should prevail over state sovereignty. The secretary-general argued that UN-armed intervention in support of this common interest was the only justifiable occasion for the use of force:

> State sovereignty, in its most basic sense, is being re-defined by the forces of globalization and international cooperation . . . [while] individual sovereignty . . . has been enhanced by a renewed consciousness of the right of every individual to control his or her own destiny. . . . Massive and systematic violations of human rights, wherever they take place, should not be allowed to stand.[24]

Admitting that a group of states had intervened in Kosovo without seeking the authority of the Security Council, Annan advocated adapting the international system to a world with new actors, responsibilities, and possibilities. He suggested that there are at least two concepts of sovereignty: individual and state.[25]

State sovereignty rests on respect for the integrity of borders. Equally, the state has a specific relation to and governance between itself and those it governs. Thus, individual sovereignty—the fundamental freedom of the individual that is enshrined in the United Nations Charter and subsequent international treaties—entails a responsibility to protect individual human beings through the practice of human security, rather than to protect those who abuse them under the guise of state sovereignty. Annan justified the use of armed force in such interventions as an action in support of the "common interest."[26]

Criteria for Intervention

1. Intervention means *more* than the use of force. Indeed, one of the primary lessons of recent military intervention is that preemptive action could have dealt more effectively and at less severe levels of impact through the simple practice of preventive diplomacy. The UN, nonetheless, has often proven slow to authorize actions and itself must change. "Humanity," according to Annan, "is indivisible."

2. Traditional notions of sovereignty are *not* the sole obstacles to effective action in humanitarian crises. How states define and defend their national interests are, in some ways, as much an impediment as the traditional understanding of sovereignty. The national interest in the post–Cold War world must change to reflect an interest that moves beyond the self-interest of the state. The *collective* interest is the national interest.

3. The Security Council itself must be able to rise to the challenge of authorizing force. If the examples of Rwanda and Kosovo illustrate anything, perhaps the first contradiction ought to lie in how the UN often fails "to find common ground in upholding the principles of its basic charter, and [act] in defense of our common humanity."

4. When the fighting stops, the *true* international commitment must begin. The commitment to fight for peace must predominate over the intent to wage war. If the tragedy of Balkan disintegration is an accurate portrait of future interventions, there appears to be far greater willingness to force formerly warring parties to terminate conflict than an ability to orchestrate the means to achieve long-term human security ends. Further, the cost of waging war in the March–June 1999 intervention in Kosovo exceeded the total cost of rebuilding the shattered infrastructure of Bosnia. Long-term, significant societal and human assistance, it should be obvious, will cost more than the amounts invested to date in the Balkans. In the future, international norms ought to focus more on means to secure such lasting peace rather than simply on how to authorize the use of force.

Source: Kofi A. Annan, "Two Concepts of Sovereignty," *Economist* (September 18, 1999) (www.un.org/Overview/SG/ kaecon.htm).

While Annan's 1999 speech was a valuable step toward the establishment of a necessary precedent—indeed an international precedent—for intervention when grossly flagrant violations of human rights occur, it did not, in the minds of some, sufficiently remove the continuing relevance of national sovereignty as a basic form of identity in relationships between states. Any number of diverse perspectives agreed on the subject of sovereignty. Chinese foreign minister Tang Jiaxuan predictably argued that national sovereignty and noninterference in a country's internal affairs are basic principles of international relations, declaring that "the outbreak of war in Kosovo has sounded an alarm for us all." Algerian president Abdelaziz Bouteflika, then representing the Organization of African Unity, proclaimed national sovereignty as "our last protection from the rules of an unjust world." Indian foreign minister Jaswant Singh held that the "state continues to have a crucial role and relevance . . . [and] therefore, [so do] national sovereignties." Oxford law professor Adam Roberts expressed concern that although the principle of intervention against obvious human rights violations was sound in principle, the "risk . . . may seem to be opening a door to lots of interventions and run headlong into national sovereignty concerns."[27]

Yet another pivotal address on the significance of Kosovo—and the most hopelessly idealistic—was made by Czech president Václav Havel to the Canadian Senate and House of Commons in Ottawa on 29 April 1999. Although the Czech Republic was one of the newest members of NATO (having joined the alliance in March 1999), the Czech people generally opposed the war in Kosovo.[28] Despite this domestic opposition, Havel unflinchingly supported the notion that the violation of human rights in any country is the business of all countries.

> Kosovo [unlike Kuwait] has no oil fields to be coveted; no member nation in the alliance has any territorial demands; Milošević does not threaten the territorial integrity of any member of the alliance. And yet the alliance is at war. It is fighting out of concern for the fate of others. It is fighting because no decent person can stand by and watch the systematic, state-directed murder of other people. It cannot tolerate such a thing. It cannot fail to provide assistance if it is within its power to do so. . . . This war places human rights above the rights of state.[29]

NATO's "humanitarian intervention" in Yugoslavia remains, nonetheless, problematic. The Kosovo intervention, after all, did not achieve a "successful outcome" until a number of civilian deaths had taken place, collateral damage occurred, and a massive air attack on the civilian infrastructure in Serbia proper was unleashed. As Charles Simic has noted, the Serbian people were also the victims of attack.

> The NATO bombing was a form of collective punishment in which innocent Serbs were made to pay the full price for the sins of their leaders who, of course, remained well protected in their shelters. In Serbia, refineries, fertilizer and petrochemical plants, factories, bridges, waterways, railroad lines, power stations, and heating plants were destroyed to make life harder on the civilians. "NATO in the sky, Milošević on the ground," a graffito in Belgrade said. With bombs dropping on their heads it was ridiculous to expect the Serbs to distinguish morally between the two.[30]

Duško Doder and Louise Branson present further evidence that in the post-Dayton environment, Serbian politicians and military officers approached the United States for help in dethroning Milošević, but the United States rebuffed them. Milošević, the "butcher of the Balkans," had helped conclude the Dayton Accord and was now regarded as a linchpin of Balkan stability.[31] The convenience of allowing a "serviceable" dictator to remain in place in the post-Dayton environment contributed directly to the chaos and manipulation that tore Kosovo apart. Thus, the idealism of NATO's humanitarian intervention was also tainted by failures of strategic policy.

PROMISES TO KEEP

While the horrendous ethnic cleansing that resulted in the worst humanitarian crisis and the largest refugee outflow from a sovereign nation in Europe since World War II may not have strictly classified as "genocide," what happened in Kosovo ought to defy comfortable definitions. (Indeed, in the Balkans, perceptions are more important than reality.) Kosovo represented sovereignty and identity for Serbs and Serbia; for Kosovar Albanians, the issue was identity, legitimacy, and external recognition.

To be blunt, it is immaterial whether the events in Kosovo constituted genocide as defined by international legal norms. For Kosovars, the agony of 1998–99 was only the most recent in a long string of historical grievances, and their refusal to accept Serbian hegemony represented a last great act of defiance. As most of them saw it, Kosovo's independence would be the only viable outcome, whether in the near or long term. By 2000, Kosovo had become an international protectorate. A less ambiguous state would have been even more fraught with danger. NATO and the West had truly entered terra incognita.

NATO's "humanitarian war" over Kosovo represented more than just its first intervention for human security, for it also chalked up several firsts of a more traditional kind. Operation Allied Force was the first sustained use of force in the alliance's half-century of existence, and the action was undertaken without the authorization of the UN Security Council. It was one of few instances of military coercion to halt human rights violations by a state against its citizens within its own borders, and it was the first instance of a strategic effect being achieved by a bombing campaign unaccompanied by sustained land operations (in this case, Milošević's capitulation and agreement to change his policy toward Kosovo).

Nonetheless, it would be a mistake to declare unequivocally that the NATO intervention established a precedent and doctrine for humanitarian intervention. Rather, a series of relevant truths suggest that any conclusions drawn must necessarily be modest. These include the reluctance of the NATO governments to risk lives, their apparent difficulty in reaching a consensus on land operations prior to the end of the conflict, the lack of will to indefinitely sustain peace-support operations once the conflict was over, and the narrow and unclear divisions about what constituted success and failure.[32]

There are two clear policy failures that led to Kosovo and the military intervention. The first occurred when American negotiators excluded the Kosovar Albanians and any discussion of Kosovo from the Dayton peace talks in order to get Milošević to agree to a solution to the Bosnian dilemma. In effect, this helped the Kosovo Liberation Army, which had been in existence since 1993, to gain legitimacy.

The second failure, which led directly to the outbreak of violence, resulted from the refusal of the West to support legitimate democratic opposition movements in Serbia and Kosovo. While Rugova's avowed pacifism seemed an attractive alternative to the standards of violence and power that dominated the Balkans in the 1990s, many Kosovars rightly concluded that the reward for non-violence was international neglect—particularly by the United States, arguably the only power that mattered in bringing about a Balkan settlement.[33]

Daniel Byman argues that the traditional governmental responses to ethnic terrorism are almost always counterproductive and only further the aims of the terrorists. In the case of Kosovo, numerous examples show how the KLA, having secured the power of NATO's military force during the March–June 1999 intervention, became the political as well as security seat of authority in the post-conflict environment. The emergence of the twenty-nine-year-old Thaqi as political leader of the sixteen-man Albanian delegation to Rambouillet, for example, was a telling reminder for a people seeking a more permanent identity as well as external recognition.[34] As the KLA demonstrated, those who secure power, even through violent means, often secure legitimacy for themselves and their cause.

Thus violence affirms identity in ethnic communities. The KLA's violent methods produced internal cohesion in Kosovo and helped secure international support. In contrast, as Byman notes, the sense of identity in communal groups that do not use violence is comparatively weak.[35] Gandhi's pacifist example in the liberation of India aside, recent incidents of ethnic terrorism and liberation show some disturbing indicators. Whether one considers Berbers in Morocco or Rugova's nonviolent "alternative" (the Independent Republic of Kosovo), groups that use nonviolent methods often do not coalesce as ethnic groups even if they have a common language, religion, and culture. Moreover, some ethnic activists argue that the refusal to use violence actually degrades and damages the cause for which a nonviolent ethnic group was promoting activism.[36]

Thus, violence creates identity. Mikica Babić, a Bosnian schoolteacher, says: "We never, until the [1992–95] war, thought of ourselves as Muslims. We were Yugoslavs. But when we began to be murdered because we are Muslims, things changed. The definition of who we are today has been determined by our killers."[37] The unfortunate paradox for governments, alliances, or international organizations that seek to effect positive outcomes in environments where ethnic terrorism takes place is that ignoring communal violence may well only further intercommunal violence. There seems, as well, an inevitability that ethnic groups will fall back to an essential ethnic identity during conflict, perpetuating a cycle of insecurity.[38]

NATO and the West were faced with a basic conundrum in March 1999. Simply put, it was this: "No matter what we do, we're going to make a mistake." Given the precedent of three years of inaction during the Bosnia debacle, the choice to intervene with military force seemed the only practical course—though not necessarily the correct one.

WAR COMES TO MACEDONIA

The spillover from the aftermath of Kosovo to Macedonia was not inevitable, although many—in hindsight—claim now that it was clearly a certainty. After all, the introduction of foreign troops into Kosovo and the apparent imminent secession of Montenegro seemed to crucially weaken the rump states of the former Yugoslavia—most especially Serbia. Given the obvious vulnerability in Serbia's southern flanks, Albanian guerilla insurgency actions began to take place north of Macedonia, centered most around the Preševo Valley in early 2000. An accompanying insurgency movement, calling itself the UÇPMB (Liberation Army of Preševo, Medvedja, and Bujanovac), now sought to "liberate" areas in the Preševo area and to recognize the gains that been made on behalf on Albanians as a result of the NATO intervention over Kosovo. (The three districts of Preševo, Medvedja, and Bujanovac were removed from Kosovo after the Second World War, while predominantly Serb areas of southern Serbia were added to Kosovo.) Thus, the UÇPMB, along with other armed groups, attempted to secure positions in the ground safety zone (GSZ), established after NATO entered Kosovo in June 1999.[39]

After the fall of the Milošević regime in October 2000, the new Yugoslav administration of Vojislav Koštunica entered into negotiations with both the UÇPMB and NATO. A subsequent agreement gave local Albanians greater rights; provided for the demobilization; disarmament, and integration of the former fighters into local security forces; and allowed Yugoslav forces back into the GSZ. The Preševo agreement, according to the Independent International Commission on Kosovo, represented a model of sound negotiations:

> The key ingredients of success were the political will on the part of
> the Serbian government to reach agreement, pressure by NATO on

the Albanian side, the involvement of both the leaders of the armed groups and local Albanians in the agreement, and trust among the various parties to the agreement. Especially important were the efforts of the Serbian government to consult and talk to a wide range of people living in the area: the bottom-up process leading up to the agreement represented a crucially important innovation of great relevance to peace agreements elsewhere.[40]

Far less optimistic observers, including high-level diplomats with significant time and experience in the region, were not as forthcoming in suggesting that quick preventive diplomacy and action could fend off further deterioration in regional security. According to one such observer,

The Independent International Commission on Kosovo (*The Follow-Up: Why Conditional Independence?* 2001), in discussing why supplies to the UÇPMB in Preševo Valley were not choked off by K-FOR, observes that both Serbs and Albanians believed it was deliberate policy: "Among Albanians, it contributes to the feeling that 'the Americans are on our side' and that it is possible to act with impunity. A much more realistic explanation, however, is the reluctance to allow peacekeeping forces to take risks. Such a large proportion of K-FOR manpower consists of 'force protection' that there are insufficient resources for public security tasks". [*sic*] The Bonn International Centre for Conversion (2001) similarly makes the point that: "Regardless of statements to the opposite, K-FOR failed in controlling Kosovo's borders with Albania, Serbia, and Macedonia. Prevention of casualties among K-FOR troops was made the highest priority . . . NATO has become the hostage of its own philosophy of running a risk-free military intervention. Erecting a protectorate means the assumption of responsibility for public security, law enforcement, and border control, or, to put it concisely, the state monopoly of violence". They also make the point that border control and security of other regional states are an explicit part of K-FOR's mandate. These are damning judgments, all the more so for being made in such measured terms.

    Force protection issues are an important part of the story, although, as we shall see, there are other mitigating factors involved. *Three observations should be made about how an overemphasis on force protection tends to appear to British eyes. The first is that it represents a missed opportunity to shape the operational landscape; if "shaping the battlefield" is an important part of American military thinking, shaping the landscape so it will not be a battlefield should also logically play a part. Secondly, it may reduce incidents in which there are casualties, but it surely increases the likelihood that if and when there are casualties they will be on a scale which assumes substantial political importance (as in Somalia in 1992). Thirdly, if one gives a force a mandate which it is then unable to carry out effectively because of tactical doctrine, this is likely to lead to confused thinking and a tendency to underestimate the seriousness of any given situation until it is too late (since the only way of reconciling the mandate and the impossibility of enforcing it is to pretend there is no problem which requires enforcement).*

However, it should be remembered that K-FOR had other substantial tasks: protecting minorities, keeping the confrontation within Mitrovica within bounds, and policing the border with the Preševo Valley during the entry of the Yugoslav Army into the Ground Safety Zone, which was not completed until early June [emphases in the original].[41]

Fueled by what we would most simply describe as a "perception discrepancy," the UÇPMB's tactical successes led some to suggest the possibility that southern Serbia itself might become destabilized and the next battle ground in the Balkans. In truth, however, the effective negotiations with the Serbian and Yugoslav governments led to quick agreement, some resolution of differences, and allowed for the effective entry of (and subsequent effective control by) the Yugoslav Army into the Preševo Valley.

As the next essay examines in more detail, the success in the Preševo Valley did not prevent the rise of the KLA (National Liberation Army) in Macedonia; to the contrary, one "success" led to the "spillover" *into* Macedonia. This phenomenon has had a number of Balkan precedents, nevertheless: success at Dayton led to the spillover in Kosovo and to the legitimization of the Kosovo Liberation Army; success in Kosovo led to the rise of the short-lived UÇPMB; success in Preševo led to a new target of opportunity in Macedonia. While analyses clearly differ about why and how the insurgency of 1999–2001, came about in Macedonia, there are some useful observations that seem commonly overlooked:

1. As the former British ambassador to Macedonia has noted in research writings, the common observation that what caused the flare-up in Macedonia was due to interethnic tensions and divisions between Slavic

Macedonians and ethnic Albanians, an equally reasonable argument could be made that the insurgency was as much about *intra-ethnic* Albanian division and rivalry as it was about the fight for civil society and more equitable distribution, administration, and justice within the Republic of Macedonia.[42] While many Web sites and analyses focus on differences between Slavs and Albanians, very few have recognized the divisions among Albanians themselves.

2. Unlike the situation in Preševo, the impact and the complexity of what happened in Macedonia took on a far more serious context. In contrast to the Serbian response to the UÇPMB, the government of Macedonia (with the support of Western governments) applied a classic counterinsurgency tactic—bombing and shelling villages where suspected "terrorists of the KLA were thought to be, and inevitably causing a cohesive backlash and rallying among the Albanian population. Further, as a result of the escalating violence, up to 120,000 people were displaced from their homes. Since the signing of the Ohrid Framework Agreement, some 50,000 refugees returned to Macedonia.[43]

3. The intra-Albanian political struggle seemed to be confirmed in polls leading up to the September 2002 parliamentary elections in Macedonia. As respected journalist Sašo Ordanoski noted in the weeks prior to the election, the popularity of the DPA (Democratic Party of Albanians) and its leader, Arben Xhaferi, suffered as a result of failed hopes and unmatched expectations in the year following the signing of the Ohrid Framework Agreement. According to preelection polls taken in July, the dominant governing political party, VMRO-DPMNE, was likely to lose to the opposition by a three-to-one margin, and Xhaferi's DPA was outstripped by Ali Ahmeti's Democratic Union for Integration, a party comprised primarily of former KLA insurgents.[44] (Notably, Ahmeti himself was the former leader of the Macedonian KLA.) Subsequent election results proved the polling data to be accurate, resulting in the ouster of both VMRO-DPMNE and DPA from the governing coalition.

4. Although commonly acknowledged in private, the degree to which criminality fueled the continued viability of the Macedonia state was a crucial factor of uncertainty. Some observers, nonetheless, have not been hesitant in their criticism. Robert Hislope, for example, claims that

crime and corruption were an important factor on the virtual state of war in Macedonia between February and August of 2001 . . . organized crime in the Albanian community is only half of the problem. The Macedonian state itself encompasses a thoroughly corrupt set of institutions that has stymied democratic development, alienated ordinary citizens, and de-legitimized the idea of an ethnically neutral, citizen-based, liberal state, especially among Albanians.[45]

Evidence from any number of sources further proves that criminal syndicates in the Balkans—concentrated primarily in Kosovo, Albania, and Macedonia—traffic 70 to 90 percent of all the heroin seized in Europe. Further evidence suggests linkages between the Kosovo Liberation Army and mafia elements, and possible linkages between the Macedonian KLA and some criminal elements. As former interior minister Ljubomir Frčkovski noted, "If you have organized crime, everything will be like in a broken mirror. You have quasi-democratic institutions, pressures in elections, guys who are totally corrupt . . . and all the money [from international institutions gets absorbed]."[46]

Ultimately, as these perhaps unforeseen and mostly unintended consequences illustrate, the effects of post-Kosovo violence spilled over into southern Serbia and Macedonia illustrated that the Balkan "Albanian Question" was far from solved. Equally, the uncertainty of the security dilemma in the south had direct effects on what happened in Belgrade.

STRUGGLING WITH FREEDOM: SERBIA AND THE FALLOUT FROM KOSOVO

We are trying to create a democratic state . . . and it takes time. Now they say you should do that which 50,000 NATO troops did not do in Bosnia.[47]

—*Zoran Djindjić,*
Prime Minister of Serbia,
assassinated in Belgrade, 12 March 2003

The prime minister's obvious frustration reflected some hard truths for Serbia in the post-Milošević era.[48] Although Milošević himself began his defense at The Hague and the ICTY (International Criminal Tribunal for War Crimes in Former Yugoslavia) on 14 February 2002—after he was handed over by Serbia following a fierce debate between Djindjić and Yugoslav President Koštunica—it seemed remarkable how Serbia seemed to listlessly pass through post-Kosovo history.[49] Lacking much of the international aid it had expected, while both suicide and employment rates remained abnormally high, Serbia seemed unable to make progress. While the international media largely (mis)focused on how Milošević's initial weeks of testimony led to soaring popularity ratings at home, the truth was a bit more complicated—and harsh. Branko Prpa, historian and widow of slain journalist and editor Slavko Čuruvija (who dared to speak out against Milošević in 1999) was direct and bitter in her assessment: "Most people don't care . . . they just don't care."

It truly was not supposed to happen this way. On 5 October 2000, the miracle had finally seemed to happen in Yugoslavia. Slobodan Milošević was apparently confident enough in his own popularity to call presidential elections on 24 September, and then to declare that a runoff would be necessary between himself and his opponent, Vojislav Koštunica, on 8 October. Yet most polling results clearly indicated that Koštunica had *won* more than 50 percent of the popular vote. This run-off, of course, never took place as a popular backlash against Milošević took place.

Koštunica himself was the candidate of a coalition comprised of eighteen different opposition parties who chose him as their joint candidate of the Democratic Opposition of Serbia (DOS). A former assistant professor of law at the University of Belgrade and ardent Serb nationalist, he remained untainted by political association with the Milošević regime. Koštunica was also unafraid to criticize both NATO and the United States for meddling in Yugoslavia's internal affairs. Both prior to and immediately after his assuming the federal presidency, he emphasized his complete lack of support for handing over Milošević to the ICTY and was reluctant to immediately release Albanian prisoners held in Yugoslavia since the war in Kosovo in 1999.

Much of the analysis that focused on Koštunica tended to emphasize his Serb nationalism, suggesting that such an attribute was a negative factor.[50] Rightly or wrongly, it was Koštunica's nationalism that proved the crucial link in not only securing command of a chaotic opposition coalition's rise to power but in securing agreements to establish parliamentary elections in Serbia on 17 December 2000.[51] Indeed, such Serb nationalism coalesced previously disparate identities: the Serbian Orthodox Church, the student resistance movement OTPOR, the Yugoslav military, and the Serbian police. General Nebojša Pavković, Yugoslavia's minister of defense and top military commander since 1998, and who had been an ardent supporter of the Milošević regime, proved especially pivotal in the dramatic—and swift—change of fortunes that took place in Yugoslavia in the early days of October 2000. Perhaps realizing that it was better to be fired than be hanged, Pavković could not deny the forces of democracy that had been unleashed and came to recognize the traditional historic role of the army as the guardian of the nation.

It seems worth noting that while Pavković, in particular, came under the heavy scrutiny of ICTY investigators, Koštunica was reluctant to suddenly dismiss key security figures during the transition period of his new administration. This was both a pragmatic and necessary move, which few in the West properly placed in context. The new Yugoslav president allowed key figures in the Yugoslav army, who had maintained pro-Milošević positions, to remain—thus securing the tacit support of the entire army. In many instances, politicians and previous key security figures simply overlooked troublesome issues with the understanding that the overall political environment needed to remain stable. Koštunica himself declared that the sudden removal of these individuals "runs counter to state interests since it inevitably leads to destabilization."[52]

It was not simply politics or pragmatism that proved to be the ultimate driving force in changing the future of Yugoslavia. In the end, it was the Serbian nation that ultimately dismembered the Yugoslav state. When, during preelection rallies, Koštunica spoke of a vision of the future Yugoslavia as a "normal, European, democratic country [in which] the government is not afraid of the people, and the people are not afraid of their government," he invoked the power of inclusion, and the "legitimacy" of democracy proved the most powerful and effective agent that engendered change.

The most evident symbol of this forceful change came not from Belgrade but from the Kolubara mine on 4 October 2000. On that day, hundreds of Ministry of Interior (MUP) policemen swept into the area to break apart a protest strike at the mine (which produces coal for half the electricity in Serbia). Rather than dispersing, the strikers appealed to the populace, and 20,000 Serbians, some coming from as far away as Čačak in central Serbia, swept into Kolubara to support the striking miners. The interior police, rather than acting to disperse the swelling crowds, simply stood aside. In that moment, the death of the post–Cold War Yugoslavia was complete and the "birth" of the twenty-first-century Yugoslavia had begun.

Whether or not the "new" Yugoslavia would survive was far from certain. Yugoslavia, after all, had gone through at least four different deaths and rebirths in the twentieth century. Yet the true agents of change were not the policymakers in Brussels or Washington. To the contrary, the true actors—and the true heroes—were the Yugoslavs themselves. Indeed, despite the massive amount of funds channeled from Washington to Serbia to support opposition movements inside the nation (as high as $77 million by some estimates), the real and significant change took place exclusively inside the borders of the state.

In the most optimistic assessment, one could say that Yugoslavia, finally, had come home to Europe. If this is true, then the architect of the "new" Europe is not Otto von Bismarck; rather, it is Georg Wilhelm Friedrich Hegel. In the death and rebirth of Yugoslavia, we may have witnessed not the return of balance-of-power politics but, far more significantly, the rise of "the march of reason in history."

Yugoslavia, nevertheless, officially came to an end less than three years later. On 14 March 2002, through a European Union initiative, the state known as Yugoslavia ceased to exist and came to be known as a loose federation known simply as "Serbia and Montenegro." (The international media, ironically, seemed to overlook this event and continued to refer to these two states most commonly as "Yugoslavia" in reporting for several years afterward.) The EU's fundamental purpose was to attempt to prevent Montenegro from declaring independence with the coercive incentive that Serbia and Montenegro would have a far better chance *together* (rather than separately) of achieving closer integration with the EU, to include eventual membership. The EU, as well as the international community, dreaded the prospect of Montenegro becoming yet another Balkan "parastate," unable to function independently yet potentially ripe for new intrastate conflict. Further, according to the EU proposal, both Serbia and Montenegro would agree to uphold their loose federation until 2005; after such time, an amicable divorce (one would hope) was possible.

The hard truth, however, remained, that Serbia in particular could not break free from the shadow of Milošević and the acceptance of guilt over what happened in Kosovo. Even the "Prudent Revolutionaries" of the new Yugoslavia could not agree to the kind of imposed collective guilt that the West seemed to demand of Yugoslavia. As one result, the lack of expected foreign and large-scale private investment never flooded in, as had been expected in the euphoria of late 2000. As Damjan de Krnjević-Mišković argued, "A country with a troubled history that remains impoverished is not a politically stable country."[53]

As for the trial of Milošević at The Hague, popularity ratings for the former president initially seemed to soar. Serbian Prime Minister Djindjić, who proved pivotal in the extradition of Milošević (partially for political expediency and also in the belief that foreign assistance would come in the aftermath), remained largely silent about the trial. Yugoslav president Koštunica, on the other hand, openly decried the trial as "hypocrisy [based on] strange nonsense."[54] Collectively, the Serbian people were far from ready to reconcile with their own past, and their own complicity, in the events of the Balkan wars in the 1990s.

On 11 April 2002, the main Yugoslav parties agreed in parliament to a new law regulating extraditions of suspected war criminals to the ICTY. A few hours after the vote, one of those suspected war criminals, former interior minister Vlajko Štojilković, stood on the steps of the Škupština (parliament), in the shadow of the great rearing black horse statues that guard either side of the staircase, and blew his head off with a handgun.

Indeed, Toma Rosandić's magnificent eighteenth-century sculptures are the exact symbol of what has happened to Serbia in recent history. Two immense rearing horses slowly crush the figures of two taut-muscled naked men, who cannot hold the weight of these stallions, or hold back their power. This, truly, was the dilemma for Serbia a half-decade after the end of the Kosovo intervention. As the pro-government newspaper *Politika* expressed it,

> The dispute on cooperation with the Hague tribunal has split our nation and ruling structure, paralyzed political life, fetters virtually every foreign policy initiative, and distracted us from the dangerous situation in which non-Serbs are maliciously rewriting our history in [The Hague] courtroom. Therefore it is necessary to do what has to be done to prevent further paralysis of our political and economic life. We have no alternative. Everybody in this conflict admits that there has been no deeper crisis since the establishment of democratic rule [in October 2000].[55]

In retrospect, several events impeded the giddy triumph of October 2000 and the high expectations that accompanied it: the debate over the extradition to The Hague of Milošević, slow economic progress and insufficient international aid, the internal power struggles between leading politicians, the eventual "death" of Yugoslavia in March 2002 and the rise of the Federation of Serbia and Montenegro, and the spillover effect from the aftershocks of Kosovo.

Although few acknowledge this truth, it is reasonable to argue that with the removal of Milošević in October 2000, the Albanian insurgency that began in Kosovo (and spread to Southern Serbia and Macedonia) initially posed a major threat to Belgrade's legitimate struggles for new democracy and peace in the region. It could, in other words, have been much worse for Serbia if the incidents in the Preševo Valley had spread like a wildfire across the Balkan landscape.

IN LIEU OF CLOSURE

The picture is not entirely and invariably bleak for the dismembered states of the former Yugoslavia and for the Balkans.[56] Slovenia, for instance, entered both NATO and the EU in 2004. (Croatia seemed to turn toward a more moderate, European-inclined stance in the first post-Tudjman elections of 2000— although domestic political events of 2002 and 2004 were not entirely promising.) Slovenia's "escape," however, from the agonizing disintegration of the Yugoslav state was facilitated by obvious differences from its former Yugoslav partners: a population that was largely ethnically homogeneous, an economy that was able to expand, and the *expectation* that Slovenians defined themselves as Europeans and not as part of the historical, cultural, or geographic landscape of the Balkans. The hard truth remains that in the wake of Yugoslavia's violent disintegration, most of the successor states faced increasing "Balkanization" by the rest of Europe. What these states needed, as Susan Woodward and Benn Steil rightly argue, was to become part of a "Europeanization" scheme. Indeed, if Europe had learned anything in the post–Cold War environment, surely one lesson would be that its economic integration actually fueled the disintegration in southeastern Europe.[57] Macedonia, in particular— through no fault or policy failure of its own—lost out on economic opportunities simply by its virtual proximity to "contaminated" Yugoslavia.

Perhaps as important as the notion of what constitutes a nation's—or a region's—security is its power. Along with the information transformation that is occurring throughout the world, reflected in the proliferation of technology, globalization, and increasing linkages among nations and regions, comes the attraction of styles of governance and openness of economic systems. In the future Europe, a nation's "soft power" (the ability to attract others to it) may be at least as important as its "hard power" (such as its economic ability to buy and to compel).

One need only look at how the attraction of EU membership has furthered compliance with expected standards of civil society, including the rights of ethnic minorities, in the Baltics and in central and southeastern Europe. One need not look much beyond how the incentive for nearer-term NATO and EU membership for Bulgaria and Romania (and even far-distant-future possibilities for Macedonia and Albania) provided cohesion and unity during the extraordinary intervention against Yugoslavia in 1999, even at the cost of great economic, social, and civil distress and expense for these nations.

In summary, there are a number of compelling and often contradictory themes that will define life "after Kosovo" not only for Kosovo, but for Macedonia and Serbia as well. The divisions between Serbs and Kosovars—and ethnic Albanians and Macedonians—will remain; there is still a need for peacekeeping forces and personnel committed to oversight; ethnic communities that employ violence will both solidify their internal identity and secure external support; and the final status of Kosovo is unclear. Despite all this, the prospects for the future are not hopeless.

Extraordinary challenges lie ahead. Even as Kosovo itself seemed intractable and unsolvable, there necessarily emerged the recognition that any strategy aimed at ending the Balkan crisis over the long haul would fail if it did not focus on the pivotal state of the region: Serbia. Any long-term, post-Milošević strategy—for both Serbia and Macedonia—simply had no choice but to focus on inclusion rather than isolation. (Indeed, the isolationist policies of the West toward Milošević during the 1990s actually helped more than harmed him.) Those in Serbia and Macedonia who sought European reintegration needed only the basic tools—and the external support—to create change.[58]

Unlike the Dayton agreement, which literally traded space for time in attempting to give the Bosnians the ability to decide their fate, Kosovo—to date—lacks any formal agreement other than UN Resolution 1244. This resolution is hardly a mandate for security sector reform, however, and—no matter what happens—negative consequences will likely ensue. While many find it unthinkable to believe that Kosovo could, or should, remain within Serbia, few sufficiently acknowledge that an independent Kosovo would immediately become a "parastate" unable to succeed or prosper on its own. Further, the Kosovars themselves must acknowledge that, in raw terms of economic geography, they cannot survive without establishing firm linkages with not just Albania, but with Serbia and Macedonia as well.

Finally, a seemingly positive event such as Kosovo's independence could cause the ultimate "spillover" effect, which, in turn, could lead to new fracturing in the Balkans. Serb secessionists in *Republika Srpska* could align with Serbia proper; Croats in western Herzegovina could claim sovereign Croatia on their territory; and Albanians in Macedonia could push for a loose confederation among themselves. Moreover, although few mention the issue these days, the Sandžak could also cause future problems for both Serbia and Montenegro.

Admittedly, such events are all worst case, but they are also possible.

As such, it seems crucial to emphasize that the war over Kosovo marked the first pivotal European event of the twenty-first century. While it may be premature to suggest that Richard Holbrooke will be remembered as his generation's Robert McNamara, it may not be as far a stretch of the imagination to recognize that Kosovo—with all its seething rage and all the necessary commitment to stem such rage—could have come to represent the Vietnam of long-term stability and support operations.[59] Ironically, any lesser level of commitment would lead to certain failure—for the region and for Europe.

NOTES

1. Although Milošević initially capitulated on 2 June, the last NATO bomb fell on Yugoslavia on 10 June; thus Operation Allied Force is sometimes referred to as the Seventy-Eight-Day War. The formal end date of the bombing campaign was 20 June. In the interim, a series of bumpy negotiations

on troop withdrawal and an agreement on status of forces in theater took place. Most notably, UK general Sir Michael Jackson refused to honor the directive of NATO's supreme allied commander, General Wesley Clark, to reclaim the Priština airport from Russian troops who had taken control of it prior to the arrival of NATO forces. Jackson retorted that he was "not about to start World War III." *New York Times,* September 10, 1999, A10.

2. *International Herald Tribune,* August 11, 1999, 1.

3. Michael Ignatieff, "The Diplomatic Life: The Dream of the Albanians. Can Richard Holbrooke Improvise an American Role in Kosovo?" *New Yorker,* January 11, 1999, 36.

4. "Slain Kosovo Farmers Autopsied as Serb Villagers Question Massacre Investigation." www.cnn.com/WORLD/europe/9907/26/kosovo.02/index.html (26 July 1999).

5. On 24 July 1999, Louise Arbour of the International Criminal Tribunal for the former Yugoslavia (ICTY) opened an investigation into the killing of these Serb farmers near Lipljan, Kosovo, after evidence indicated that the act was ethnic cleansing committed by Kosovar Albanians. (Arbour had also opened separate investigations against NATO for alleged criminal actions during the air campaign.)

6. *New York Times,* September 13, 1999, 5.

7. Michael Mandelbaum, "A Perfect Failure—Kosovo's Consequences Were Just the Opposite of What NATO Intended," *Foreign Affairs* 78, no. 5 (September/October 1999): 2.

8. The seeds for the Kosovo provisional government were sown at the 1999 Rambouillet negotiations in France. Immediately following Milošević's capitulation in June, the provisional government made claims to legitimacy by establishing town councils, setting up police forces, and claiming authority—and responsibility—for Kosovo's reconstruction.

9. Chris Hedges, "Kosovo's Next Masters?" *Foreign Affairs* 78, no. 3 (May/June 1999): 42.

10. Ibid., 41; *New York Times,* June 25, 1999, A1. Thaqi, whose Albanian name is Gjarpni, denied all allegations that there had been systematic executions of KLA members. He earned a reputation, however, for not allowing dissent among subordinates. In June 1997, a Kosovo Albanian reporter, Ali Uka, who had close links with the KLA, was found dead in his apartment in Tirana, Albania. Uka's face was disfigured with multiple stab wounds from a screwdriver and the edge of a broken bottle. At the time of his death, Uka had been sharing his apartment with Thaqi.

11. Hedges, "Kosovo's Next Masters?" 42; Christopher Layne and Benjamin Schwarz, "For the Record," *National Interest* 57 (Fall 1999): 10.

12. The KLA also successfully co-opted Rugova's League of Democratic Kosovo. Establishing close links within the organization, many LDK leaders took up weapons, in defiance of Rugova's pacifism, and organized village units when the rebellion erupted. By 2000, the apparent successor to

Rugova was Ramush Haradinaj, who had significant support from the Albanian diaspora in Europe. Notably, Haradinaj did not fare well in the October 2000 elections in Kosovo and was himself under indictment and investigation by the ICTY.

13. Some attention rightly focused on President Bush's 1992 "Christmas Warning" to Milošević, in which the United States threatened military action in the face of continued Yugoslav repression of Kosovars. Despite this threat, Milošević long believed that he had the right and freedom to act as he chose fit in Kosovo.

14. Ignatieff, "Dream of the Albanians," 34; Scott Anderson, "The Curse of Blood and Vengeance," *New York Times Magazine,* December 26, 1999, 34. Admittedly, other forms of arms flow occurred, such as from organized-crime trafficking, the Serbian black market, and the capturing of Yugoslav weapons.

15. Stacy Sullivan, "From Brooklyn to Kosovo, With Love and AK-47's," *New York Times Magazine,* November 22, 1998, 50–57.

16. Isa Blumi, "Kosovo: From the Brink—and Back Again," *Current History* (November 2001): 374.

17. P. H. Liotta and Anna Simons, "Thicker than Water? Kin, Religion, and Conflict in the Balkans," *Parameters: U.S. Army War College Quarterly* 28 (Winter 1998–99): 11–27; Anderson, "Curse of Blood and Vengeance," 30.

18. Noel Malcolm, *Kosovo: A Short History* (New York: New York University Press, 1998), 17–19.

19. Serbian extremists murdered Gjeçov in 1929. Four years after his death, the *kanun* was published as a book.

20. William W. Hagen, "The Balkans' Lethal Nationalisms," *Foreign Affairs* 78, no. 4 (July/August 1999): 62.

21. Liotta and Simons, "Thicker Than Water?"; Chuck Sudetic, *Blood and Vengeance: One Family's Story of the War in Bosnia* (New York: Norton, 1998).

22. During his regime, which lasted from 1945 until its collapse in 1991, Hoxha was particularly brutal regarding the *kanun.* Those found guilty of committing a blood killing were buried alive in the coffins of their victims.

23. Anderson, "Curse of Blood and Vengeance," 34.

24. *Christian Science Monitor,* September 29, 1999, 7.

25. Kofi A. Annan, "Two Concepts of Sovereignty," *Economist.* www.un.org/Over view/SG/kaecon.htm (18 September 1999).

26. Ibid. Admittedly, Annan would not define the common interest other than to insist that armed intervention should be based on "universal legitimacy," such as a Security Council mandate. "What is the common interest?" he asked rhetorically during his UN address. "Who shall defend it? Under whose authority? And with what means of intervention?"

27. *Christian Science Monitor,* September 29, 1999, 1–7.

28. Polls taken during the intervention showed that only one-third of the Czech populace supported the NATO action against Yugoslavia.

29. Václav Havel, "Kosovo and the End of the Nation-State," *New York Review of Books,* June 10, 1999, 5.

30. Charles Simic, "Anatomy of a Murderer," *New York Review of Books,* January 20, 2000, 29.

31. Duško Doder and Louise Branson, *Milošević: Portrait of a Tyrant* (New York: Free Press, 1999). This claim is not without merit. In 1996, a National Security Council member privately remarked to one of the authors that Milošević, unlike other Balkan politicians involved in the Dayton talks, was "a serviceable villain" and a "worthy Shakespearean opponent."

32. Adam Roberts, "NATO's 'Humanitarian War' over Kosovo," *Survival* 41, no. 3 (Autumn 1999): 120.

33. James Hooper, executive director of the Balkan Action Council, argued that the European allies deeply resented how American negotiators largely ignored them at the 1995 Dayton peace conference. At Rambouillet, therefore, the Europeans took a more visible role and sought to project a more equal partnership with the United States on Balkan security issues. During private discussions with American diplomats involved in the Rambouillet peace conference, however, one of the authors received the (admittedly American) perspective that the European diplomats simply confused and complicated the negotiation process, virtually assuring a failure to secure a definite outcome. If this is true, future complementarity between European and U.S. negotiators (and policy makers) on security issues of mutual concern may well be thorny. Indeed, the 2003 dispute within Europe, and between Europe and the United States over war in Iraq seemed to bear this out. James Hooper, "Kosovo: America's Balkan Problem," *Current History* (April 1999): 161.

34. The designated political leader at Rambouillet at the outset of talks, however, was not Thaqi, but Jakup Krasniqi.

35. Daniel Byman, "The Logic of Ethnic Terrorism," *Studies in Conflict & Terrorism* 21, no. 2 (April/June 1998): 156.

36. Ibid.

37. *New York Times,* July 28, 1995, quoted in Chaim Kaufmann, "Possible and Impossible Solutions to Ethnic Civil Wars," *International Security* 20, no. 4 (Spring 1996): 144.

38. Liotta and Simons, "Thicker Than Water?"

39. According to the Independent International Commission on Kosovo report titled, "The Follow-Up: Why Conditional Independence [for Kosovo]?" (available at www.politikforum.de/forum/archive/22/2002/11/3/22835), this "Ground Safety Zone" was intended to separate NATO forces from Yugoslav forces, and only lightly armed Serbian and Montenegrin police were allowed to enter.

40. Ibid.

41. E-mail addendum, dated Tuesday, 16 July 2002, 9:14 A.M., from Mark Dickinson (British Ambassador to Macedonia from 1997 to August 2001), to a paper written while in residency as a fellow at the Weatherhead Center for International Affairs, Harvard University, titled "A Teacup in a Storm: Two Crises in Macedonia, 1999–2001." Used with permission.

42. Dickinson, Section IV, "Interlude, 1999–2000," 1.

43. Independent International Commission on Kosovo report, 7–8.

44. Sašo Ordanoski, "Macedonia: Special Forces 'Election Threat,'" Institute for War and Peace Reporting *Balkan Crisis Report*, no. 351, 19 July 2002, available at http://www.iwpr.net.

45. Robert Hislope, "Organized Crime in a Disorganized State: How Corruption Contributed to Macedonia's Mini War," *Problems of Post-Communism*, 49, no. 3 (May/June 2002): 33–41.

46. From an interview with Hislope, quoted in essay, 36.

47. Quoted in Tim Judah, "Review Essay," *Survival* 44, no. 2 (Summer 2002): 159.

48. This frustration, of course, was both internal and external. Externally, the international community gave little or no visible support to Serbia and Montenegro prior to Djindjić's assassination. Following his death and the massive internal crackdown on organized crime within Serbia, reforms within the nation led the international community to lend more direct support. On 16 June 2003, the United States "recertified" Serbia and Montenegro as cooperating with The Hague War Crimes Tribunal section. Ironically, it took the prime minister's death before any actual diplomatic, economic, or political support was forthcoming. In 2004, U.S. aid—in the amount of $110 million—was threatened to be withheld from Serbia because of claimed intransigence on the apprehension of indicted Balkan war criminals.

49. We note here that there was clearly no love lost between Yugoslav President Koštunica and Serbian Prime Minister Djindjić. Although both had aligned in the multiparty coalition that defeated Slobodan Milošević, the differences between the two clearly emerged under the new government, most especially regarding the extradition of Milošević to The Hague. Koštunica, a pragmatic former assistant law professor at the University of Belgrade whose translation into Serbo-Croatian of the American *Federalist Papers* decades earlier has become a classic textbook in universities, and a staunch advocate of "the rule of law," proclaimed the extradition to be a farce and had virulently opposed it. Djindjić, the skillful politician and former mayor of Belgrade, had rammed through the Serbian parliament the legally questionable extradition of Milošević, partially in the expectation that increased international assistance (particularly American) would follow. (It did not.) The ultimate showdown between the two came in the Serbian presidential election of Fall 2002. Whoever won that contest won

ultimate political control over Serbia. As 2002 came to a close, however, the apathy of the Serbian people was clear. Two runoff elections, during which Koštunica twice won the overall vote for the Serbian presidency, still resulted in failure. (Serbian law requires 50 percent of the population to vote and in both runoff elections the total percentage voting fell short of the mark.)

50. The most stridently negative assessment of Koštunica can be found in Norman Cigar, *Vojislav Koštunica and Serbia's Future* (London: Saqi Books/The Bosnian Institute, 2001), with a forward by Sonja Biserko. Cigar, a professor of strategic studies at the U.S. Marine Corps Command and Staff College, clearly views Koštunica with distaste, arguing that his policies, through reliance on institutions like the Orthodox Church and the army, sought to maintain a destructive Greater Serbian perspective and prevent reconciliation with neighboring states, and thus impede regional stability. In essence, Cigar implies that Koštunica is little better than Milošević. Such implication, nonetheless, is sheer hyperbole.

51. Koštunica, following the October 5, 2000 "revolution" in Yugoslavia, was installed as the federal president of the Yugoslavia republics of Serbia and Montenegro. Until Milošević was elected by the Yugoslav parliament to the federal presidency in 1997, this position was little more than a figurehead. In theory, at least, Milošević's socialist party still controlled the parliament of Serbia and republic offices following the 5 October events. The relative ease with which Koštunica called for and received agreement on December 17 parliamentary elections in Serbia only demonstrated how completely Milošević had lost control of power.

52. John Schindler, "Yugoslav Revolution under Threat," *Jane's Intelligence Review,* January 2001, 18–20.

53. "Serbia Prudent Revolution," *Journal of Democracy* 12, no. 3 (July 2001): 110.

54. "Serbian Analysts: Serbs a Long Way from Reconciliation with Their Past," Radio Free Europe/Radio Liberty *Balkan Report* 6, no. 10 (22 February 2002). Djindjić argued that since The Hague Tribunal was largely seen as a puppet of the West, political opposition within Serbia would only increase, thus making it even harder for Serbia to hand over additional suspected war criminals and to impose economic reforms that are the prerequisite for more rapid integration with Europe. For a slanted though informative view of the Milošević trial, see Joseph Lelyveld, " 'The Defendant': Slobodan Milošević's Trial, and the Debate Surrounding International Courts," *New Yorker,* May 27, 2002, vol. 78, no. 13: 82–95. For frequent updates on the trial, including archival reference, free subscription is available through the Institute for War and Peace Reporting at https://www.global-list.com/secure/ iwpr/subscribe_pop.asp, under "Tribunal Updates."

55. Dragoslav Rančić, *Politika,* 3 April 2002, reported in *World Press Review* (June 2002): 41.

56. In the late 1990s, a Slovenian military officer, in a private conversation with one of the authors about ethnic cleansing, said that Slovenia "took care of that problem centuries ago." While the assertion is untrue, the remark is astounding in its implications. If ethnic homogeneity is the basic ingredient for European membership integration, along with a superior and indeed racist attitude by the "included" group toward "excluded" ethnic groups (such as Serbs or Muslims), then the entire future European security architecture may well be based on fraud. A 1997 European Union poll revealed that almost one-third of all Europeans—and more than 40 percent of all Austrians—considered themselves "racist" and intolerant of minority ethnic groups in their own countries. Despite this recognition, Europeans have collectively put pressure on themselves and future EU partners to foster ethnic tolerance and acceptance. Jörg Haider's resignation from the Freedom Party coalition in the Austrian government in 2000 indicates that Europe expects openness and not xenophobia, and nominally fosters tolerance rather than indifference.

57. Benn Steil and Susan L. Woodward, "A European 'New Deal' for the Balkans," *Foreign Affairs* 78, no. 6 (November/December 1999): 97–98.

58. In retrospect, casting blame on Serbia alone for Kosovo was problematic. As William Hagen emphasizes, the West should not have been surprised by how and why events progressed as they did in the last decade of the twentieth century in the Balkans. At Rambouillet, the United States and its allies proposed terms threatening Milošević with loss of Serbian control over Kosovo and its 90 percent Albanian-speaking majority following a referendum to be held after three years. This amounted to accepting, in return for nothing of importance, a crushing national loss that would have delegitimized any Serbian government. It is hard to imagine why the United States or the other NATO powers expected Milošević to acquiesce. More caustic observers, particularly the journalist Tim Judah, reject this claim as "much-touted nonsense . . . beloved of Milošević's Western apologists." The issue was—and the argument remains—a bit thornier than that. Alan J. Arrington, a military attaché at the Court of St. James during the 1999 NATO intervention, argued forcefully (shortly after his retirement) that the bombing of Kosovo was unnecessary, because Milošević, through diplomatic channels, had conceded on all the major issues in contention prior to 24 March 1999 (Alan J. Arrington, "Clinton Had a Chance to Avoid Kosovo Bombing," *Colorado Springs Gazette,* October 12, 2000).

59. The subsequent 2003 intervention in Iraq, nonetheless, is, in retrospect, a far more serious, daunting, and complex problem.

Cry, the Imagined Country: Legitimacy and the Fate of Macedonia

Among the people of the Balkans and the Caucasus they tell the legend of a captive eagle that manages to escape from captivity and return to his family. But his master had ringed his claws, and this stigma makes the fugitive a stranger among his own race. The family refuses to take back their own.

—*Ismail Kadaré*[1]

As tragedies go, the first six months of the twenty-first century proved fundamental for the fate of Macedonia, and perhaps for the future of European security as well. Admitted as an "associate member" of the European Union in April 2001—with the mutually proclaimed expectation of eventual EU membership—Macedonia was also a member of the so-called "Vilnius Nine" seeking membership in the next enlargement round of the North Atlantic Treaty Organization.[2] Yet among this group of ex-Communist states seeking NATO membership (widely seen as less restrictive than EU criteria for membership), both Macedonia and Albania were regarded as having little to absolutely no chance of securing NATO membership during the Prague summit of 2002.

Within Macedonia itself, an ethnic Albanian insurgency, under the rubric of the National Liberation Army (NLA), came perilously close to paralyzing the nation in a state of political and civil "lock up"; equally, the leaders of NATO, the European Union, and the United States seemed paralyzed about what—if any—course of action was best to take regarding the fate of this tiny ex-republic of former Yugoslavia.[3] Ultimately, even the ethnic governing coalition within Macedonia, formed in May 2001 and proclaimed a "national unity government," appeared incapable of agreement on central, critical issues. One informed observer caustically remarked, only days after the unity government's formation, that "this government has nothing to do with genuine democracy . . . [and] is too weak and fragile to undertake any serious reform in the country."[4]

Despite such obvious flaws and essential contradictions, however, we argue here that Macedonia's future is essential to the future European security architecture. Indeed, whether or not Macedonia survives will largely be dependent on "external" forces—as with the situation in all the former republics of ex-Yugoslavia. Unlike many other analyses that have focused on the Balkans, and former Yugoslavia in particular, and argued that the causes for conflict and disintegration are markedly similar, we suggest that Macedonia's problems are unique. It remains a too common and crucial mistake to assume that the root causes for disintegration that have plagued Serbia, Croatia, Kosovo, Montenegro, Bosnia-Herzegovina, and Macedonia since 1991 are all linked to a few centrally identifiable factors. Nothing, in fact, could be farther from the truth. With the exception of attempting to lessen the disparate economic geographies that continue to spell promise or peril for the entire region, the root solutions for southeast Europe will prove problematic, and at times seem overwhelming, but will not prove impossible.

The answer to whether or not the future Europe will be characterized as one of constant security dilemmas or a place of integrating security identities may well lie in the fate of Macedonia. To date, the limited responses and commitments on the part of external parties have not been entirely promising. During the time of the intense crises in March 2001, a confidential e-mail passed to the authors from Skopje portrays in stark detail the security conundrum that Macedonia had now entered:

> ———, who is a member of the [Macedonian] National Security Council, consulted me this morning about the legal possibilities

and implications of introducing either a state of emergency or state of war in the country (neither is possible according to our 'democratic' constitution, by the way) . . . He also told me about the last night's meeting with the ambassadors of NATO countries in Macedonia. . . . Our leadership was shocked to hear accusations [directed at] the Macedonian government and suggestions, such as: "This is your internal problem and we have nothing to do with that." . . . The only country that CAN do something in regard to Albanians is the USA . . . and after seventy-eight days of illegal bombings [in Kosovo, Serbia, and Montenegro] they now insist on their non-existing legal mandate to help Macedonia. . . . Macedonians already speak about territorial division of the country just to avoid war. . . . Albanians are voluntarily going into the UÇK (National Liberation Army) while Macedonian youth flee the country and try to avoid mobilization. I assume that a big problem will be my city, Skopje, which is at the same time the largest Macedonian and Albanian city in the world. . . . I just had coffee with a Bulgarian diplomat in Skopje and his observation was that no Macedonian is willing to defend and to die for the country. Everybody thinks about fleeing the country, including me.

Despite the dark fatalism of the above commentary, however, a small window of opportunity still existed in southeast Europe. This essay seeks to consider that opportunity, highlight significant historical markers that define the region, outline some of the differences and grievances that have plagued Macedonia throughout its tenuous post-1991 existence, emphasize what initiatives have thus far been undertaken, and offer pathways that might prove useful in outlining possible solutions to the political and civil nightmare that took hold of Macedonia in 2001.

THE WEIGHT OF TOO MUCH HISTORY

In the Balkans, a common aphorism suggests that the region "has so much history, it doesn't need a future." It seems worth noting, nonetheless, that in terms of historical geography, the term *Balkans* is itself an imaginary destination. German geographer August Zeune mistakenly named the Balkan peninsula (*Balkan Halbinsel*) at the beginning of the nineteenth century to avoid the culturally sensitive euphemisms of "the European part of Turkey" or "Turkey in Europe."[5] Zeune suggested that the northern borders of the region were the Balkan mountains in Bulgaria, and although Zeune's geographical boundaries were drawn too narrowly it remains true that for much of its history since the time of Roman frontier (*limes*) the Balkans was the fault line of empires, religions, and civilizations where people clashed in their various roles as guardians of the "imaginary" border.[6]

Nowhere in this region is imaginary geography more profound than in Macedonia, where the burden of the past leans into every human effort made toward building the present. Indeed, Macedonia and its surrounding area are so rich in history that it seems criminal to summarize in a few pages. Despite the claim by some that Macedonia is simply a "Tito-ist creation" of post-1944 Yugoslavia, the nation itself has a long, illustrious—and weighted—heritage.

Time of the Ottomans

After the fall of Czar Samuil's kingdom in 1014 and the subsequent fall of Byzantium (in 1453), the next great—and most enduring—regional influence was that of the Ottoman Empire.[7] The empire itself reached its peak during the middle of the sixteenth century, and covered the Balkan Peninsula, Romania, a significant part of Hungary, all of the Aegean Islands, Cyprus, Algeria, Tunisia, Libya, Egypt, Syria, Arabia, Mesopotamia, Asia Minor, Georgia, and Crimea.[8] Although a still contentious claim, by most accurate accounts the Ottomans practiced religious tolerance. With the exception of the recruitment for the Janissaries and early Islamization, for the most part, the Turks conducted very little proselytizing, although many Albanians, and Slavic speaking people did convert to Islam.[9] The Turks believed that religion corresponded to nationality, which was the basis of their *milyet* system. Non-Muslims throughout the Ottoman Empire enjoyed autonomy and religious freedom as long as they accepted the Sultan's sovereignty. The Slavs in Macedonia were ruled by their fellow Slavs, who in turn were subject to Turkish governors. Political rights, however, were reserved for the Turks, but ironically, "religious toleration made possible the self perpetuation of national consciousness."[10] Ackerman describes Ottoman rule similarly: "However repressive and exploitive, Turkish rule was also a time of peaceful coexistence. Turks, Slavs, Albanians,

Greeks, Vlachs, Jews, and Roma often lived together in multiethnic communities."[11]

As the Ottoman Empire declined during the late nineteenth century, Macedonia became an inevitable pawn in European balance-of-power politics. After the Russo-Turkish War of 1878, Macedonia became part of Bulgaria as a means to counter Austria-Hungary. Four months later at the Congress of Berlin, Macedonia was ceded back to the Ottomans. To counter Turkish rule, the Internal Macedonian Revolutionary Organization—known most commonly as IMRO— emerged in 1893.[12] (Indeed, Goce Delchev, one of the 1893 founders of the Internal Macedonian Revolutionary Organization—*Vnatreshna Makedonska Revolutsionna Organizatsiya*—is a symbol of liberation from Ottoman Turks for *both* Bulgaria and Macedonia.)

Dimitrija Čupovski, in a 1913 article, describes the thirty-five years between the Congress of Berlin and the Balkan Wars as "one bloody page of continuous struggle of the Macedonian people for their liberation." Between 1898 and 1903, there were 400 Macedonian-Turkish confrontations. Multiple European press reports confirmed the terror and violence conducted by the Turks on Macedonians during the nineteenth century;[13] equally, Rebecca West in *Black Lamb and Grey Falcon* describes the subsequent reprisal activities of IMRO in the region as the most effective "terrorism" in Europe.

The Kruševo Republic

In August 1903, a Macedonian uprising resulted in the attempted establishment of the fabled Kruševo Republic. Although the "republic" lasted only two months and ended in defeat, its significance is recounted in Macedonia's present constitution. That 30,000 rebels held off a formidable 300,000 Turkish force and established a democratic commune of the Kruševo Republic was in itself an ultimate act of defiance against the Ottoman Empire.[14] The Republic lasted less than two weeks. In a "Manifesto" reportedly issued by its leaders to neighboring Muslim villages, Kruševo's temporary government declared its tolerance of differences in "religion, nationality, sex or conviction." Although widely celebrated within Macedonia, the politics of history in the Balkans have served to marginalize the Ilinden Uprising and the progressive agenda embraced by at least some of those involved.[15]

Two World Wars, Two Balkan Wars, a Great Disaster, and a Civil War

The First Balkan War (1912–13) resulted in Macedonia's and Albania's "liberation." The Second Balkan War in 1913, however, ended in Macedonia's division: one-tenth to Bulgaria (Pirin Macedonia), one-half to Greece (Aegean Macedonia), and two-fifths to Serbia (Vardar Macedonia).[16] World War I resulted in another Macedonian division, but by the end of World War II—and with Josip Broz Tito's direct forethought—Macedonia became a recognized republic, with a distinct ethnic identity and recognized Slavic language, within the Yugoslav federation.[17]

In contrast to the emerging Macedonian nation, a "greater" Albanian nationalism was the among the last to develop among the Balkan peoples. In 1878, the Prizin League was established to protect Albanian lands, and it would later challenge Ottoman rule. Albanian guerrilla units emerged in 1906, and in 1908, Albanian leaders adopted the Latin alphabet for the Albanian language. In 1910, the Albanians revolted against the Ottomans in Priština, and the revolt spread to Kosovo, and in 1912, Albanians took over Skopje. The Treaty of Bucharešt in 1913 established the Albanian state; however, almost half the Albanian population lived outside its borders.[18]

After World War I, Vardar Macedonia and Kosovo became part of the Kingdom of the Serbs, Croats, and Slovenes, but Albanians were never recognized as a separate nation. Macedonia was known as *South* Serbia and Kosovo as *Old* Serbia. The Serbs suppressed the Albanians, which in turn fostered Albanian armed resistance in the 1920s and raised Albanian national awareness among Albanians.[19] Further complicating the blurred distinctions of cultural, historic, and ethnic geographies, the "Great Disaster" of 1922 in Asia Minor—in which Mustafa Kemal's forces permanently pushed the Greek population out of Anatolia and burned Smyrna to the ground—led to the exchange of populations between Greece, Bulgaria, and Turkey in 1923. Thus, most of the Greek refugees from Asia Minor replaced the Slavic and Turkish elements in Greek Macedonia (an area that Slavic Macedonians commonly refer to as "Aegean Macedonia"). Much of the once predominant—and Slavic—population of Greek Macedonia moved north to present-day

Macedonia and Bulgaria. Thus, Kemal (who in 1934 assumed the name of Atatürk) laid the foundation for the modern Turkish state with his brilliant campaign of 1921–22; his actions affected the dynamics of Macedonia as well.

After Tito's break from the Cominform and Stalin in 1948, relations between the Albanian state and Yugoslavia rapidly worsened, making life for Yugoslav Albanians often unbearable. Yugoslavia closed down Albanian schools and discriminated against ethnic Albanians politically, economically, and socially. Albanians began identifying themselves as Turks simply to escape this discrimination.[20] As a counterbalance to this growing unrest, Marshall Tito emphasized a strong "Macedonian" identity in the Macedonian republic as a way to contain Albanians within Serbia and Macedonia; equally, Tito reneged on an earlier promise (made during the Partizan struggle of World War II) to help foster an Albanian state that united the entire Albanian population. The ethnic Macedonian population increased within the Yugoslav Republic of Macedonia as Greek Macedonian refugees fled from the Greek Civil War (1946–49). Macedonia's state apparatus gained more authority when the Yugoslav 1974 constitution decentralized the party and state administrations' activities for all the republics. Furthermore, the constitution reinforced Tito's contrived borders, which enhanced his own divide and conquer tactics, and the Yugoslav National Army served as the protector of Yugoslavia's unity. Tito's death unraveled all these efforts, and Yugoslavia became subject to eight political parties and eight fiefdoms.[21]

The National Liberation Army

Events in 2001 in Macedonia turned the state's, region's, and world's attention to the actions of the National Liberation Army (NLA), a self-appointed protector of Macedonia's ethnic Albanians. The NLA was a transnational organization, with many of its commanders veterans of the *Ushtria Çlirimtare e Kosovës*—more commonly known as the UÇK or the Kosovo Liberation Army (KLA). Many observers have confirmed that during the Kosovo crisis of 1999, members of the KLA included ethnic Albanians from Macedonia. Most prominent among these was Ali Ahmeti, the leader of the

NLA until 2001. He was raised in the city of Kičevo, Macedonia and became politically active while studying at the University of Priština in Kosovo. His participation in a 1981 street demonstration landed him in Idrižo prison for a year. In 1993, Ahmeti and Emrush Xhemajli gained the approval of the Nationalist Movement of Kosova to create the KLA.[22] By 1997, Ahmeti was living in Tirana, and actively organized groups to infiltrate and attack police in Kosovo. At the time, his uncle, Fazli Veliu, actively assisted him, and by 1999, they had established the NLA. Just as there were reports of arms smuggling from Macedonia to Kosovo earlier, there were reports in 2001 of arms smuggling from Kosovo to Macedonia.[23] Further reporting indicated active transnational efforts that coordinated a clandestine logistics network within Macedonia in support of the KLA.[24]

Western analysts believed that the NLA had 1,500 members. The NLA recognized that any forceful overreaction by Macedonia would play to the NLA's advantage. Some observers believed that the NLA actions were a result of frustration by the ethnic Albanian extremists in Kosovo based on the recent elections in Kosovo that produced a moderate local government under the leadership of Ibrahim Rugova. Until the spring of 2001, the confrontations between Macedonian government forces and the NLA had taken place in Tetovo (with a 90 percent ethnic Albanian population) and in other border towns in the northwest that were largely ethnic Albanian. By April 2001, however, with the active control of Kumanovo, in the northeast, the tide of events clearly had taken a turn for the worse. By June 2001, rebel forces had seized Aračinovo, six miles from the capital of Skopje and within rocket-firing range. The precarious "national unity government"—a coalition of four political parties that included two ethnic Albanian identities—weakened considerably in credibility when the leaders of the two Albanian parties, Arben Xhaferi and Imer Imeri, signed a joint declaration of support with NLA leader Ahmeti in Priština on 22 May.[25] At the time the declaration was signed, Boris Trajkovski, president of the Macedonian republic, and NATO Secretary-General George Robertson openly referred to the NLA as "criminal, thugs, and terrorists."

Clearly, the need for external, active EU and NATO intervention within Macedonia grew obvious. Admittedly, as events worsened by the summer of 2001, both the EU and NATO attempted more proactive approaches. On 5 July 2001, NATO mediated a ceasefire between Albanian insurgents and Macedonian government forces; whether or not such mediation would lead to permanent resolution or prolong ambiguous outcomes, however, remained uncertain.

BIRTH OF A NATION

On 8 September 1991, Macedonia held a referendum addressing the establishment of an independent Macedonian state. The ensuing vote overwhelmingly favored independence. Notably, the vote was extended to Macedonians who lived outside the Macedonian state. This extension of votes uncovers a current debate, which is the tension between a citizen of the Macedonian state and a member of the Macedonian nation, and the obligation of a citizen of a state versus a member of a nation. The constitution reflects this tension as well. It refers to constitutional nationalism, which confers a special status for the dominant nation within the state versus the democratic principle that confers sovereignty on all citizens of the state.[26] The constitution stated:

> Taking as starting points the historical, cultural, spiritual and statehood heritage of the Macedonian people and their struggle over centuries for national and social freedom . . . and particularly the traditions of statehood and legality of the Kruševo Republic . . . as well as the historical fact that Macedonia is established as a national state of the Macedonian people, in which full equality as citizens and permanent co-existence with the Macedonian people is provided for Albanians, Turks, Vlachs, Romanics and other nationalities living in the Republic of Macedonia, and intent on the establishment of the Republic of Macedonia as a sovereign and independent state, as well as a civil and democratic one.[27]

Gjorge Ivanov, an ethnic Macedonian and long-time proponent of the creation and sustainment of civil societies, argue that the constitution's preamble allows for other nationalities, thus making it a "civil and democratic state . . ." and that

> The Slav population in the Republic of Macedonia and its Macedonian national identity has always been both [an] ethnical and political or civil one. There are no contradictions for the

Macedonians in this regard. As for the Macedonian Albanians, demanding their loyalty to the State is a problem in terms of the necessity to overbridge the gap between their ethnic origin and political reality in Macedonia.[28]

From a contrary perspective, ethnic Albanian party leader, Nevzat Halili suggests that "What we need are radical changes in the Macedonian Constitution. Albanians in Macedonia should be recognized as a constitutive people. There are three categories of citizens in Macedonia. Macedonians are first-class citizens, Albanians are second class, and Serbs and others are third class."[29]

According to the disputed 1994 census, Macedonia's population was just over two million people, with 66.6 percent Slav Macedonians, 22.7 percent ethnic Albanian, 4 percent Turkish, 2.2 percent Roma, 2.1 percent Serb, and 2.4 percent of other minorities. Ethnic Albanians of Macedonia, however, insisted that they comprised 40 to 50 percent of the population.[30] Notably, the U.S. Department of State gives Macedonia (a coalition-led parliamentary democracy) high marks for maintaining an independent judiciary, freedom of the press, and a system that "generally [respects] the human rights of its citizens."[31] While the State Department praised the government for its handling of over 335,000 ethnic Albanians from Kosovo during the 1999 NATO intervention, the refugee crisis clearly strained political relations. Slavic Macedonians feared that Kosovars would permanently remain in Macedonia, thus significantly shifting ethnic balance within the country.

Strained relations between ethnic Macedonians and ethnic Albanians have existed since the birth of the Macedonian state.[32] Albanians boycotted the referendum on Macedonia's independence and the 1991 census, claiming the latest census would not portray their true percentage of the population. By 1993, however, the ethnic Albanian Party for Democratic Prosperity (PDP) declared that Albanian autonomy was not on its agenda. Instead, the PDP wanted state and constitutional recognition of the Albanian nation.[33] The on-going university dispute concerning the Albanian university in Tetovo and the flying of Albanian flags on administrative buildings in Tetovo and Gostivar resulted in police intervention and three Albanian deaths in July 1997. These deaths unfortunately were only precursors to the far greater unrest that visited these areas in 2001.

The PDP's desire for partner-nation status springs partially from the Albanian claim that their ancestors predated the Slavs as Macedonian inhabitants, that Albanians peacefully coexisted with many minorities, and that they constitute the largest minority in Macedonia. In practical terms, partner-nation status would establish joint decision-making mechanisms at the state and local levels; proportional representation on the police force, the military, the judiciary, and other such institutions; and rights such as the state-sanctioning of Albanian language, education, and flag. Slav Macedonians insisted, nonetheless, that Albanians were treated equally as evidenced by the political participation of Albanian parties and leaders. Furthermore, partner-status may have led to a Bosnia-like situation with spillover effects from Kosovo. Albanian leader Arben Xhaferi was correct in his assertion in 1999 that only 3 percent of this Albanian population was employed in the public sector, armed forces, courts, media, and cultural organizations.[34]

Given the historical context of ethnic relations in Macedonia, one must differentiate between Kosovar Albanians and Macedonian Albanians. From its start, Macedonia, unlike Serbia under the reign of Milošević, had always intended an inclusive regime. In Macedonia, Albanians were included in state politics; in Kosovo, Albanians in the 1990s set up parallel—and illegal in the eyes of the Yugoslav government—"shadow" institutions. Albanian political parties in Macedonia have been instrumental government coalition partners. Between 1992 and 1998, the PDP served in a government coalition of Branko Crvenkovski, head of the then Social Democratic Union of Macedonia (SDU). After 1998, the Democratic Party of Albanians (DPA) joined the government coalition of the Internal Macedonian Revolutionary Organization-Democratic Party of Macedonian Unity (IMRO-DPMNE) and the Democratic Alternative (DA). In May 2001, the fragile "national unity government" comprised four previously competing parties: the Social Democratic Alliance of Macedonia (SDSM), under the leadership of Tito Petkovski and Branko Crvenkovski; Xhaferi's DPA; the Albanian Party for Democratic Prosperity (PDP); and the Internal Macedonian Revolutionary Organization (IMRO) under Ljupčo Georgievski.[35]

The splits within the PDP manifested this diversity of opinion within the Albanian community; after several splits producing the

Party for Democratic Prosperity of Albanians (PDP-A) under the leadership of Arben Xhaferi and the National Democratic Party (NDP), Xhaferi emerged as the prominent political leader. Notably, it was the increasingly nationalistic tones of regional neighbors, Albanian President Sali Berisha and Kosovar Albanian leader Rugova, that fostered the splits within the PDP in Macedonia.

In general principle, effective governing coalition required leaders willing to compromise and foster dialogue to tackle the challenges of a newly democratizing state, especially if that state seeks legitimacy from all its people. While the "national unity government" of Macedonia in 2001 appeared to profess such legitimacy, the ethnic tensions between Slavs and Albanians often replicated themselves in the governing coalition's internal struggles for power. In 1998, however, when Ljupčo Georgievski, declared hard-line Slav nationalist leader of the IMRO, included Arben Xhaferi and his party as a coalition partner, Xhaferi expressed moderation of his previous stance: "We can find common ground for ethnic integration through mutual understanding."[36] In truth, both Georgievski and Xhaferi's moderate stands differed from past rhetoric. Vasil Tupurkovski, leader of the Democratic Alternative (DA) observed, "They [IMRO and DPA] realized perfectly well they could never have won with the radical positions they used to hold, and they really wanted to win, and to hold power."[37]

The 1998 coalition was not the first expression of moderation. In 1994, voters learned that they could make a difference in the political system, and they rejected IMRO's nationalist agenda. Instead, voters elected a coalition of the Social Democratic Alliance of Macedonia (SDSM), the Socialist Party of Macedonia (SPM), the Liberal Party (LP), and the Party for Democratic Prosperity (PDP). Under the leadership of then Macedonian president Kiro Gligorov, the coalition maintained a pragmatic approach to its foreign and domestic policies.[38] The government skillfully managed relations with Serbia, Albania, Greece, and Bulgaria, and maintained an accommodative approach toward Macedonia's ethnic Albanian population.

This 1994 election result came after Macedonia's first multiparty elections in 1990 that produced a nationalist coalition under the leadership of the IMRO. A twenty-four year-old poet, Ljupčo Georgievski, led the IMRO, and he articulated four aims: first, Macedonian independence; second, withdrawal of the Yugoslav National Army and the establishment of the Macedonian Defense Forces; third, an independent currency; and, fourth, world recognition as a sovereign state. IMRO's message was that Macedonia was for Macedonians, which was not widely received by Macedonia's ethnic minorities.[39] Fortunately, other points of view were represented. For example, the SDSM pushed for a compromise solution with Yugoslavia such that Macedonia would have autonomous status as a Yugoslav republic.

Moreover, because the 1990 elections did not produce a majority, the government created a panel of experts, who had little party affiliation; this panel was designed to facilitate good governance that reflected compromise. Three ethnic Albanians were included on this panel, an early indication of the government's accommodation through power sharing. With the nationalist coalition's slight majority, Gligorov was appointed as president, while Georgievski was named vice president. An economics professor, Nikola Kljuŝev, became prime minister. This form of power sharing reflected the polls of the day.[40]

Escaping the Balkan Whirlpool

An April 1991 poll in Macedonia indicated that 60 percent of the citizenry favored a restructured Yugoslavia as opposed to Macedonian independence. In principle, the values of toleration and diversity appeared to be important elements to the people and leaders of Macedonia. (Unlike the examples of breakaway former Yugoslav republics, Slovenia and Croatia, many believe that Macedonia would still be part of the Yugoslav Federation if not for the clumsy maneuverings and often ruthless machinations of the former Serbian leader Miloŝević.)

Until 2001, Macedonia's political accommodation helped avert the ethnic conflicts and disasters experienced by its regional neighbors. Ethnic parties influenced the governing coalition agenda. In June 1993, a constitutionally directed institution, the Council of Interethnic Relations, was created. The thirteen-member council, with representatives from six ethnic groups, was charged with studying interethnic issues and making recommendations to Parliament. While its influence was questionable, it was a forum for dialogue.[41] Further, the influence of the council was felt in Robert Badinter's proposed new "draft" constitution, written during the 2001 crisis.

Creating Community

Macedonia's political leadership proved a significant factor in Macedonia's relative ethnic harmony. In 1995, President Gligorov talked about the citizens of his nation in this manner: "We are all Macedonians. We are all citizens of this country and Albanians have a long-term interest to integrate themselves in this country. This does not mean that they should lose their national, cultural and linguistic characteristics." Furthermore, he stated that:

> In the ethnically-mixed Balkans, it is impossible to create compact national states in which only members of one nation can live. This is an absurdity which can hardly be realized in Europe. . . . Perhaps one nation can win a victory here and there, but then this would only lead to revanchism on the part of the others, and thus, there would never be an end [to warfare].[42]

One way to defuse the problem of conflicting nationalities is to create a new nationality or identity. Indeed, the idea of creating a European identity in Macedonia influenced Macedonia's desire for membership in European institutions. The idea of a federalized Europe resonated with citizens of Macedonia; citizens were accustomed to a federalized system under the former Yugoslavia, and viewed their inclusion in the European family as a way to bolster their status and way of life. In truth, some ethnic Albanians did feel Macedonian. Nusret Jakupi, a military officer in the Macedonian army claimed: "I, as an Albanian, feel I am in my country. I haven't come from another country. I am living in the same place where my grandfather, my great grandfather, and generations before have lived."[43] According to an ethnic Albanian leader, Sami Ibrahami

> I think we have been lucky to establish this country without any conflict at all. And the contributions of [the ethnic] Albanians were a huge part because we know that we can talk to each other. The dialogue is going on in Macedonia. That is our priority. We respect each other, but the promises that are given are not realized. It was always said that things would be realized step by step but unfortunately there's still not a real democracy here. But we have continued to preserve the peace. If we have not learned the lessons from Bosnia-Herzegovina then we are illiterate.[44]

Gligorov suggested as well that balance must be achieved to win legitimacy from not only ethnic Albanians, but also from the majority, Slavic Macedonians:

> It's not possible to implement overnight a maximization program because there are other political entities in the country that have to accept those solutions. Two-thirds of the population in Macedonia are [Slavic] Macedonians, and one-third consists of all the [other] ethnic groups together. Therefore, if you want to improve some of the ethnic rights, then you have to convince the [Slavic] Macedonian population that that is good, and that it is to the benefit of the country and of the [Slavic] Macedonians of the nation. All this requires time, preparation, argumentation, patience.[45]

It seems that by first acknowledging overlapping identities and political communities, the state can better know how to foster legitimacy from the diverse population.

Polling Specifics: Indications and Warnings

Polls conducted from March to May of 2000 supported Gligorov's concern of attaining legitimacy among all ethnic groups. Perhaps ironically, ethnic Albanians seemed to have more confidence in the Macedonian government than Slavic Macedonians did. Based on polls conducted in April 2000, political preferences had changed since the 1998 elections. The governing coalition (IMRO-DPMNE and DPA) lost public support, but that loss was mainly among Slavic Macedonians. Ethnic Albanians, however, increased their support for the coalition and particularly showed increased support for DPA over PDP.

The main opposition party, SDSM, doubled its public support since the 1998 elections. This support was mainly from the Slav Macedonian and other-than-Albanian ethnic communities. SDSM supporters also tended to have more urban, educated, and higher economic status than supporters of IMRO-DPMNE. Specifically, ethnic Macedonians increased their support of SDSM from 15 percent to 27 percent, while their support of the IMRO-DPMNE coalition declined from 16 percent to 13 percent. Ethnic Albanian support had grown for DPA from 31 percent to 50 percent, yet decreased for PDP from 32 percent to 13 percent. President Tra-

jkovski received positive support from ethnic Albanians (62 percent) and mixed support from Slav Macedonians (46 percent).
Prime Minister Ljupčo Georgievski, also from the IMRO-
DPMNE, received more favorable support from ethnic Albanians
(54 percent) than from ethnic Macedonians (37 percent). The
overall declining confidence in the ruling coalition may be attrib-
uted to events in Kosovo, a presidential election scandal, and poor
economic performance. The leaders of the SDSM party,
Tito Petkovski and Branko Crvenkovski, were gaining Slav
Macedonian support while losing ethnic Albanian support. Former President Gligorov, whose views were in line with
IMRO-DPMNE, continued to have great support among Slav
Macedonians (72 percent) and limited support among ethnic
Albanians (15 percent). Arben Xhaferi enjoyed widespread support among ethnic Albanians (83 percent) and minimal support
from Slav Macedonians (21 percent).[46]

What did these polls mean? First, Gligorov seemed to enjoy
support based on his leadership. Even though his views reflected
the views of the ruling coalition, the declining support for that
coalition did not affect him. It appears that he enjoyed great
power vis-à-vis his prime ministers during his time as president.
Under Trajkovski, the powers of the prime minister vis-à-vis the
president seemed more balanced.[47] Second, Slav Macedonians and
ethnic Albanians were clearly not homogeneous in their opinions.
Slav Macedonians tended to split between the IMRO and SDSM,
while there were also several Albanian parties. While the DPA
gained increasing Albanian support, it was a party that reflected
political accommodation and moderation. Further, ethnic Albanians gave Slav Macedonian President Trajkovski great support.
This seemed to be the beginning of crosscutting cleavages where
political parties reflected issues that overrode previous ethnic
agendas.

Other indicators show that there was a decline in support of the
police and army in both ethnic communities. However, ethnic
Albanians increased their support for the judicial system from 7
percent to 20 percent favorable and for both the national, rising
from 24 percent to 50 percent, and local governments, now at 51
percent from the previous year's 38 percent. Slav Macedonians,

however, showed less support for the national government, declining from 46 percent to 27 percent, and the local government, dropping from 38 percent to 29 percent. Moreover, each community's views toward each other changed. Ethnic Albanians' view of Slav Macedonians had improved from 17 percent as very favorable to 44 percent very favorable. Overall, 76 percent responded as either very or somewhat favorable. Only 30 percent of Slav Macedonians viewed ethnic Albanians as either very favorable or somewhat favorable. Only 9 percent of ethnic Albanians and 20 percent of ethnic Macedonians felt that ethnic relations were very bad and could result in a grave crisis. Moreover, both groups strongly backed a united Macedonia (ethnic Albanians at 82 percent and ethnic Macedonians at 99 percent). Finally, 30 percent of Albanians only identified with their ethnic group, and 50 percent viewed themselves as an ethnic Albanian and then as a Macedonian citizen. Slav Macedonians viewed their residency in Macedonia as the most important factor of their identity (55 percent), followed by town (12 percent), occupation (13 percent), nationality (13 percent), and religion (5 percent).[48]

These polls also reflected increasing legitimacy for the government among the ethnic Albanians and even increasing tolerance toward others—important criteria for a liberal democracy. The polls, again demonstrated the importance of the government's ability to elicit legitimacy from all communities, even among the Slav Macedonians showing declining support for the government. These polls also suggested crosscutting societal cleavages based on how people perceive themselves and others. State loyalties seemed to be present and could help form the basis of a widespread civic identity; these loyalties and identity might form the basis of a cohesive political community at the state level. Clearly though, polarized sentiments remained.

Another set of polls indicate that ethnic Albanians appeared more optimistic about the economy than ethnic Macedonians, with 65 percent of Slav Albanians optimistic concerning the arrival of Western economic aid than Slav Macedonians (34 percent). However, both ethnic Albanians and ethnic Macedonians tended to favor the market economy with some restrictions. Overall, 77 percent of the public was in favor of private versus state ownership of small

businesses, and 58 percent were in favor of foreign investment. Supporters of IMRO-DPMNE and DPA tended to support the free market more than supporters of SDSM. Slav Macedonians viewed trade
(26 percent), foreign investment (26 percent), and fighting
corruption (16 percent) as the top economic policy priorities, and
ethnic Albanians relatively agree, with foreign investment (31 percent),
privatization (23 percent), trade (14 percent), and fighting corruption
(12 percent).[49] In addition, both communities considered unemployment as their top election issue.[50]

Polling Data: Implications

The political process still held promise as a viable alternative to
ethnic violence. As was increasingly evident up to the crisis of 2001,
the DPA easily asserted itself in government, seeking to attain better
job and bank loan access for Albanians. In addition, ethnic Albanian
politicians in Kosovo did not publicly declare support for ethnic
Albanian extremists; they did, however, warn of Western support for
their Slavic rivals. Macedonia's neighbors also declared support for
the fledgling nation. Albania reaffirmed its commitment to respect
Macedonia's borders and rejected any call for a Greater Albania.
Greece and Bulgaria offered military support to assist with border
security between Macedonia and Kosovo.[51]

Further, DPA rejected the extremist goal of a Greater Albania,
and even Deputy Prime Minister Ibrahami claimed that Albanians
can live in several countries, just as German-speakers live in Ger-
many, Austria, and Switzerland.[52] The NLA, however, challenged
Xhaferi's DPA political efforts, and in response, Xhaferi pressed for
more rapid improvement concerning ethnic Albanian rights using the
political process.

To be blunt, most Albanians just wanted stability and opportunity, and they had no desires for a Greater Albania. In effect, the sense
of an Albanian "nation" that crosses over territorial borders did not
necessarily demand the creation of a separate Albanian "state." Generally, Albanians wanted their language officially sanctioned; more
decentralization, constitutional amendments guaranteeing equality; a
change in the preamble of the constitution; an internationally moni-
tored census; and an Albanian language university. The EU's common

security policy chief, Javier Solana, thus frequently discouraged the use of force from all sides and encouraged Trajkovski to step up negotiations. In particular, Solana noted that Macedonia's democracy was strong enough to not *require* direct international mediation for its political dialogue. Solana observed: "Xhaferi is part of the government."[53] In retrospect—and as the NATO-brokered ceasefire of 5 July 2001 illustrates—Solana was overly optimistic in his assessment.

According to Nikola Dimitrov, then Macedonia's national security advisor (and later Ambassador to the United States), "This is a fight against terrorists, not against any single ethnic community." An ethnic Albanian villager called the government attacks against the NLA "a tragedy and a crime." He also added that the Albanians want "only justice" and not a separate state.[54] Branko Geroski, the editor of *Dnevnik* [the Daily], Macedonia's largest newspaper, the Macedonian state sanctioned language status for the Albanian language and a change in the constitution's preamble that clearly articulated equal citizenry status for all people were imminent. The state, with the OSCE's help, accredited a new university, albeit not the Tetovo University, with Albanian as the primary language.

THE ECONOMIC GEOGRAPHY OF MACEDONIA

Because this case focuses on the central identity and legitimacy of the Macedonian state, it seems crucial to recognize that neither language and religious differences nor the resolution of ethnic Albanian-ethnic Macedonian relations would prove sufficient to understanding the "insecurity" of the region. Far more significant tensions exist. Specifically, it was the success or failure of Macedonia's *economic* geography that would ultimately determine the fate of its physical geography. It adds to the tragedy of Macedonia to emphasize that, although the methods are clearly abhorrent, the central criticisms of the NLA—as well as the claims of the ethnic Albanian political leadership—were essentially correct.

Xhaferi, in particular, long emphasized this opportunity disparity and just as strongly emphasized that the key to Macedonia's potential fatal weakness was in its economic geography. With some justification, Albanians regularly complained that they were the victims of systematic discrimination in Macedonia, receiving the worst health care and education and having the least chance for employment in the public sector. As Xhaferi would have it, any potential future success would be compelled by the inevitable allure of the West. Inequality between ethnic identities, however, only described part of the problem. Macedonia suffers from—and has always suffered from—severe economic inequities in the Balkans. The poorest of the former Yugoslav republics, Macedonia, was born economically "challenged."

While Macedonia is seemingly well understood as a precarious example of potential Balkan instability, the tiniest nation in southeast Europe is also a poorly understood success. Opposing political identities, economic inequities, and regional conflict would seem to have preordained doom long ago for the tiny nation-state. Yet, remarkably, Macedonia was able to balance extraordinary contradictions.

In April 1993, the UN recognized the republic named "the Former Yugoslav Republic of Macedonia"; EU members and the United States followed, and China, Russia, Turkey, Bulgaria, Slovenia, and Croatia recognized the new state with its chosen name, Republic of Macedonia. Greece's economic embargo against Macedonia and the lethargic international recognition hurt Macedonia's economy; lack of recognition prevented receipt of foreign loans and capital.[55] Once the compromise name, Former Yugoslav Republic of Macedonia (FYROM), was approved by the UN, the country was finally able to join the International Monetary Fund and attain observer status in the Conference on Security and Cooperation in Europe (CSCE).

Macedonia suffered both from Greece's embargo and from the UN blockade imposed on Serbia (Macedonia's main trading partner). Six weeks into the Greek blockade, the economic "cost" for Macedonia was $80 million per month, an estimated 85 percent of its total export income. By 1994, the anti-Yugoslav blockade had cost Macedonia $3 billion.[56] Accounting for the pressures of the 1999 Kosovo crisis, some estimates suggest that Macedonia's lost economic benefits since independence were as high as $8 billion.

Further compounding such pressures, the regional demographic shifts that occurred during 1999 must also be considered as part of the economic geography of the region. Macedonia allowed 12,000 NATO troops to deploy along the Kosovo border without, initially, having any guarantees of Macedonia's internal security should the nation have been brought into a wider conflict. Although widely criticized in the international community for not providing more support to the hundreds of thousands of Kosovar Albanians that fled across the border from Yugoslavia, few recognized that Macedonia was simply *incapable* of handling such a flow of human traffic. Georgievski managed to survive the storm, however temporarily. One central goal of his government's policy, nonetheless, seems to have had little chance of a reality in the near term: Macedonia's acceptance into NATO membership.

It must be recognized that the 1990s radically altered the economic geography of the Balkans, shifting economic processes to focus on new markets and new partnerships. The region's legacy of a turbulent past, it marginal position at the periphery of Europe, and the lack of any economically dominant country willing to act as a driving force for the region simply assured continued underdevelopment.[57] In truth, such potential leading states, such as Slovenia and Croatia, were pulled by the "soft power" allure of the European Union and readily sought to economically escape from the Balkans. According to Simić, both Slovenian and Croatia viewed regional Balkan initiatives with mistrust; further, in January 1998, Croatia adopted constitutional amendments that prohibited return to any form of "Yugoslav" community.[58] Some feared that a new "Golden Curtain" would replace the former Iron Curtain; in other words, economic strength would replace totalitarian authority as a form of control.

Unlike Slovenia or Croatia (former Yugoslav republics that had some forms of economic infrastructure and liberalization tendencies in place at the time of their respective beginnings as independent states), Macedonia possessed economic geography challenges from the beginning. A nation whose largest external export was traditionally fermented tobacco, Macedonia continued to face daunting internal and external challenges. In retrospect, it ought to seem miraculous that the tragedy of 2001 did not arrive sooner.

Critics of the argument presented here will point to milestones established by the Stability Pact for Southeast Europe, as well as milestones that were reported to the White House by the U.S. Department of State, which clearly dictate a methodology and roadmap for assessing strategic progress.[59] Such milestones, to be blunt, were bureaucratic "paper tigers" and sidestepped reality. The international community—however politically insensitive the claim is—suffered from an acute case of "Yugo-fatigue." By some admittedly large estimates, reasonable reconstruction estimates for the Balkan nations affected by war reached an astounding level of $100 billion required by 2004.[60] Even with the Balkan Stability Pact of 1999, investment would not—and could not—approach such a high level and thus the consequence of war and its aftermath would affect both the Balkans and Europe for decades to come. Yugo-fatigue and political inertia thus partially explain the less than halfhearted attempts in 2001 to assist Macedonia in its most severe crisis since its independence.

DEMOCRACY, LEGITIMACY, AND STABILITY

At a National Endowment for Democracy forum in Berlin during the Summer of 2000, then Secretary of State Madeleine Albright discussed the importance of southeastern Europe, which faced the forces of globalization, fragmentation, and democratization:

> First, democracy may be the most stable form of government in the long run, but in the short run it is among the most fragile. The leaders of new democracies are often required to implement dramatic economic and political reform in countries with little democratic tradition and a host of inherited problems. In such situations, democratic processes must be relentlessly nurtured, for their success cannot be assumed. Second, as democracy has spread, truly global cooperation on its behalf has become possible. However, [globalization] has also made democracy more vulnerable in more places. Southeastern Europe is a prime example. So our new Community of Democracies will begin life with much work to do.[61]

Equally, Gjorge Ivanov highlighted the importance of liberal democracy, namely, the significance of substantial democracy over procedural democracy:

> The problem to organize a normal dialogue is within each ethnic group. That is why political leaders should be diplomats rather than pragmatic politicians. They should know how to negotiate and to respect the counter partner because democracy is not a matter of procedure but it is a substantial as it depends on the participants

themselves [note his earlier emphasis on the citizenry]. Procedure is also essential but not as much as it is with homogeneous societies.[62]

One must be careful, though, not to haphazardly apply lessons from one case to another, recognizing that key differences are just as important as discovering important similarities.

A key challenge in this case is understanding and analyzing the nature of the NLA. While movement did occur on the political and civil front in Macedonia, however glacially it appeared to do so, some form of police action had to be taken against the NLA. In essence, it was the escalation of violence between Macedonian forces and the NLA that fueled the increasing polarization of Slavs and Albanians in 2001. The NLA, a nationally marginalized group, increasingly gained the sympathy of the Albanian citizenry through an agenda of violence.

The NLA was a phenomenon that seemed to have evolved from the KLA. While many within the diaspora Albanian community in particular would object to our assertion, we consider the NLA to be a transnational, terrorist organization born from the grievances of the Albanian community within Macedonia and from the "successful" Albanian experience in Kosovo that led to the liberation of the province from the control of Yugoslav President Slobodan Milošević. The uncomfortable "lesson" of the Kosovo experience led the NLA and its supporters to believe that abuse of "human rights" in the Balkans would eventually cause the West to intervene. One of the obvious falsehoods of the NLA experience in Macedonia, nonetheless, was that it remains impossible to establish a *viable* civil society at the point of a gun. At best, the legitimate Albanian grievances within Macedonia would be offset by the use of NLA violence to secure its political and civil agenda.

Unlike the 1995 post-Dayton Bosnia-Herzegovina and Croatia, and Kosovo of post-1999 intervention, Macedonia, despite all its challenges and contradictions, had not yet been "cleansed." Macedonia was the last genuinely multiethnic state in the Balkans. For some, this suggested the impossibility of its continued existence.

It still serves to emphasize that Macedonia is the *last* ethnically heterogeneous society remaining from the former Yugoslavia. While some seasoned Balkan observers, notably Timothy Garton Ash, have argued that the true lesson of post-Yugoslavia is that ethnically homogeneous societies—such as Slovenia—tend toward stability rather than disintegration, any number of philosophers and social scientists have argued the exact opposite. A nation, as Franck has noted, largely comprises a people, while a state consists of its citizenry and bounded territory.[63] Only rarely does a nation of one people find itself within the exclusive territory of a defined boundary in a "pure" nation-state. Historic attempts to create a "pure" nation-state have not established happy precedents: Heidegger's self-perceived task of helping the German *Volk* find a "home for itself" contributed to the appropriation of *völkisch* symbols by Adolph Hitler and his movement of National Socialism. Similarly, one motivation for ethnic cleansing by Bosnian Serbs lay in the desire to create the identity of the *Republika Srpska*.

Hegel, notably, argued forcefully that ethnic diversity was both a *necessary condition* and a *necessary product* for the stability of the modern state.[64] Indeed, as Hersh has suggested, Hegel foresaw a "general system" of state stability based on the bond of the *polis* rather than allegiance secured by blood bonds. Further, as a precursor to the liberalist movement of the twentieth century, Hegel stated repeatedly that for a state to be "rational," it must be pluralistic.[65] Although Isaiah Berlin was largely critical of Hegel's "Utopianism," he supported Hegel's advocacy of pluralism and multiethnic identities, claiming that "subjection to a single ideology, no matter how reasonable and imaginative, robs man of freedom and vitality."[66] Berlin echoes Hegel's earlier concerns in warning of the dangers of monoethnicism:

> This is the beginning of nationalism. . . . If each culture expresses its own vision and is entitled to do so, and if the values and goals of different societies and ways of life are not commensurable, then it follows that there is no single set of principles, no universal truth for all men and times and places. The values of one civilization will be different from, and perhaps incompatible with, the values of the other. If free creation, spontaneous development along one's own native lines, not inhibited or suppressed by the dogmatic pronouncements of an elite of self-appointed arbiters, insensitive to history, is to be accorded supreme value; if authenticity and variety are not to be sacrificed to authority, organization, centralisation [*sic*],

which inexorably tend to uniformity and the destruction of what men hold dearest—their institutions, their habits, their form of life, all that has made them what they are—then the establishment of one world, organized on universally accepted rational principles— the ideal society—is not acceptable.[67]

COOPERATION OR CONFLICT: THE END IS IN SIGHT

> In this part of the world it is difficult to find the true path between reason and emotion, myth and reality. This is the burden of the Balkans, which prevents us from becoming truly European.
> —*Kiro Gligorov*

Macedonia, since its independence, has come perilously close to internal collapse on more than one occasion. Geographical isolation, obvious lack of technological sophistication as well as lack of access to technology, and evident and continuing political instability— severely aggravated by the Kosovo crisis of 1999—failed to encourage foreign investment over the long run. That said, such investment along with the successful implementation of economic reforms are the only means to secure stability or ensure Macedonia's long-term success.

If one were to take a retrospective look at the Balkans in general, it might indeed seem miraculous that Macedonia had not suffered a fate similar to that of its neighbors. The future for Macedonia seems laced with promise as much as peril.

Given the argument presented here, however, we offer the following observations as plausible future directions:

Macedonia Will Always Be Defined by "The Other." Distasteful as it seems, Macedonia owes perhaps a debt of gratitude to Slobodan Milošević. If not for his ruthless machinations and maneuverings, Macedonia may well not have had the impetus to seek independence. If not for the clumsy manueverings and often ruthless machinations of the former Serbian leader, the amount of international support for Macedonia's independence and continued success would have been even smaller than it was. Macedonia, nonetheless, will likely continue to be defined by its relations with other states that surround it. Whether we speak of Kosovo or Serbia at large, Greece, Bulgaria, or Albania,

Macedonia—a landlocked country—must gracefully maneuver a path through difficult waters.

Recent polls indicated that ethnic Albanians support NATO and feel more secure with NATO troops in Macedonia. Slavic Macedonians did not, however, favor a NATO presence in the Macedonia, and half had an unfavorable view of the United States. VMRO-DPMNE supported NATO presence in the FYROM, but SDSM did not. However, Slav Macedonians responded favorably to joining NATO, with perhaps the hope that NATO membership could help secure economic benefits. Confidence in the EU, UN, and OSCE had also gone down from 1999 to 2000 among Slav Macedonians (41 percent to 33 percent, 44 percent to 34 percent, and 42 percent to 30 percent, respectively). Ethnic Albanians, conversely, consistently held these organizations in high regard (82 percent, 79 percent, and 85 percent).[68]

Macedonia's Dependence on "The Kindness of Strangers." According to the Stability Pact for Southeastern Europe Coordinator Bodo Hambach, regional support for Macedonia would override the conflict of 2001. His view was that the NLA "terrorists" were politically isolated "as never before, from the government of Albania, from the official Kosovo Albanians, and from the political parties of the Albanians in Macedonia." When asked in an interview "Who is supposed to keep in check these UÇK (NLA) fighters from Kosovo?" Hambach replied:

> Whoever holds power in Kosovo. And that is K-FOR. It has the obligation under international law to ensure that no threat to a neighboring country comes from this territory. K-FOR has to draw a line in the sand. . . . Not all violence shown on TV means war. We are dealing with armed confrontations, but these are not crossing the threshold of war. I consider it a controllable conflict. This includes clear opposition terrorism. . . . These terrorists now notice how isolated they are. They now want to present themselves as freedom fighters and portray the terrorist actions as a popular uprising in Macedonia. . . . Since Milošević's departure there has been no head of state in the region who considers military aggression to be a means of policy.[69]

Interstate cooperation also occurred between Serbia and Macedonia. Both countries agreed that the best way to manage the ethnic Albanian extremists was with restraint. Presidents Trajkovski and Koštunica signed treaties that delineated the border between their countries. Furthermore, Koštunica rejected the idea of a Greater Serbia and believed that political accommodation would produce a future stable and decentralized Yugoslav state.[70]

The Need to Establish Milestones for Determining Economic Progress and Promoting Achievements. The sad truth, of course, is that it took war in Kosovo before renewed assistance would be offered in any significant amount to Macedonia. As with Bosnia, the tragedy of a neighbor's agony provided another form of salvation both for the Macedonian people and for the viability of its continued existence as a state. Until 1999, again unlike Bosnia, the presence of UN forces in the area paled in comparison to the wide latitude of authority and responsiveness that NATO and S-FOR exercised in post-Dayton Bosnia. The Balkan Stability Pact—known more formally as the Stability Pact for Southeast Europe—signed by Macedonia in June 1999, provided the opportunity for both economic and significant material assistance to this struggling nation. The pact thus provided a measure of hope, however small, for the future republic of Macedonia. Yet no effective milestones existed, as part of a formal process, to demonstrate how the pact itself fell farther and farther behind in implementing the change it was originally intended to stimulate.

A separate and serious issue concerns the smuggling between the Macedonian and Kosovo border. With unemployment high at 32 percent, and many unemployed Slavic Macedonians unenamored with ethnic Albanians (including the NLA) attaining wealth through illegal activities, namely smuggling, the situation remained tense. The good news was that Macedonia had been able to curb inflation, obtain $250 million of Greek investment, attain a budget surplus, and foster job-creating investments. The continued path toward economic prosperity thus helped defuse potential ethnic tensions.[71] Further, Greece and Bulgaria volunteered to patrol the border, which could help thwart the smuggling activities.

The Necessity to Create an Effective Public Relations Program, a Long-Term Vision, and a Definitive Strategy. Macedonia continued to be "defined by the other" player in the political dynamic. Perhaps just as crucial as working to improve ethnic Slavic and Albanian relations and opportunities and for establishing a sound economic base, Macedonia portrayed a viable political identity to the expanding and transforming Europe. If Macedonia had serious intention to eventually become part of the European Union—and it should be clear that this was a long-term goal—then an effective and clear communication of the nation's intent to become *included,* rather than continually excluded, had to be part of the long-term vision. The signing of the Stabilization and Association Agreement and an Interim Agreement between Macedonia and the European Union on 9 April 2001—in the midst of NLA attacks in western and northeastern Macedonia—was a promising first step.[72] The economic benefits of increased EU integration may have best ameliorated the collective lot for the Macedonian population, which according to polls, were most worried about their economic plight. If the nation had made viable economic progress, perhaps the ruling coalition would have regained support.

A Pragmatic Policy that Seeks Wider Support for Contributions Already Made and Yet to Come. Macedonia received obvious neglect from the West during the years of its early independence. Treated largely as a staging area for NATO operations both prior to, during, and after the Kosovo engagement of 1999, it remained unclear how firm the West's security, economic, and even political commitments to Macedonia's future success were. Such ambiguity, while providing the West with a means to escape culpability, also invoked an inevitable bitterness in the Macedonians themselves.

Resist Accommodation Based on Ethnic Difference. Macedonia is the last genuinely multiethnic state in the Balkans. For some, this suggests the impossibility of its continued existence. While partition seems the easiest—and most viable—solution, it will prove not to be a solution at all. Macedonian president Trajkovski was sincere in declaring that "We cannot redraw borders and boundaries, making smaller units of even purer ethnic states. We cannot survive as a region if ethnicity becomes the sole defining justification of statehood."[73] Partition would only forestall deeper root causes that will surface once again in the future. This is perhaps the lesson we have yet to learn from the effective partitioning of Bosnia-Herzegovina into three entities and in creating the protectorate status of Kosovo within Yugoslavia.

Promote Europeanization. If Europe has learned anything in the post–Cold War environment, surely one lesson was that European economic integration actually *fueled* disintegration in southeast Europe.

Outsiders push Balkan integration . . . but such efforts are doomed to fail in the face of local insecurity and political resistance. The Balkans need the leverage that can be achieved only by satisfying the region's single common aspiration: "Europeanization" . . . In practice, Europeanization means extending the cross-border monetary, trade, and investment arrangements that already operate within the EU across Europe's southeastern periphery. . . . What the region is not achieving politically on an intraregional basis can therefore be achieved within a few years under the aegis of Europeanization. This "New Deal" should apply to all states in the region—Albania, Bosnia, Bulgaria, Croatia, Greece, Hungary, Macedonia, Romania, Slovenia, Turkey, and Yugoslavia—with no state's existing EU affiliations jeopardized or set back through participation. . . . Early staged entry into liberal European economic regimes will encourage private-sector development, reduce the state's economic role, underpin the rule of law, and increase the benefits of forswearing violent conflict over resources and national boundaries.[74]

The desire to join Europe can be a regional unifying factor. One need only look at how the attraction of EU membership has furthered compliance with expected standards of civil society, to include the rights of ethnic minorities, in the Baltics and in central and southeast Europe. One need not look much beyond how the incentive for nearer-term NATO and EU membership for Bulgaria and Romania, and even far-distant-future possibilities for Macedonia and Albania, provided cohesion and unity in the extraordinary intervention against Yugoslavia in 1999, even at great economic, social, and civil distress and expense within these nations.

What are the strategic implications for American and European policies?

First, policymakers must realize that the ambiguity that professed neutrality between contending parties cannot be maintained indefinitely. Second, there is a pressing need to link Macedonian identity with other European identities and organizations. Membership in NATO, for example, now appears to be a cultural marker of inclusion and economic attractiveness as much as a security guarantee. Since EU membership criteria are difficult to fulfill, NATO membership is the next best thing—a "Good Housekeeping" seal of approval that assures security guarantees and makes a region more attractive for outside investment. Finally, policy makers must acknowledge openly—while a window of opportunity still exists—the necessary commitment it will take to assist in southeast Europe.[75] Civil societies, both creating and sustaining them, require difficult choice and *focused* effort.

In truth, Macedonia has received little credit or acknowledgment for its success since independence but is always faulted for its failures. No matter how difficult the choices for the people and for the region itself, it is no accident that the Macedonian question of the nineteenth century has been resurrected in a new form in the twenty-first century and requires a frank assessment of this nation's necessity and probability for survival.

There is a pressing need to be specific and blunt about the fate of Macedonia. If the "international community"—admitting that the term itself is worthy of lengthy separate debate—supports the legitimacy of Macedonia as a state, then there is a direct responsibility to more firmly anchor that state's future. Whether or not one subscribes to a pragmatic *Realpolitik* or supports a more optimistic sense of increasingly linked European security and integration agenda, one stubborn truth remains: Macedonia cannot achieve success on its own. If the major players who will most affect the outcomes in the Balkan region (the Russian Federation, the EU, NATO, and the United States) cannot find some means of mutual accommodation and agreed to strategy, then the future Europe will quickly prove itself to be the perfect fraud. For those who honestly believe in the notions of democracy, civil society, economic integration, and common security, the choice is clear. It is time for the Balkan eagle to lose the stigma of its own "ringed claws."

NOTES

1. "The Balkans: Truths and Untruths," in *The Southern Balkans: Perspectives from the Region,* ed. Dimitris Triantaphyllou, *Chaillot Papers* 46 (Paris: European Institute for Security Studies, 2001), 5–6.

2. The seven other Vilnius Nine members included Bulgaria, Romania, Slovenia, Slovakia, Estonia, Latvia, and Lithuania. Croatia later joined the NATO Membership Action Plan (MAP) process. In 2002, all applicants—with exception of Albania, Croatia, and Macedonia—received invitations to join the North Atlantic Alliance.

3. For simplicity, the acronym NLA or the term *National Liberation Army* is used consistently in this work to represent rebel Albanian forces inside Macedonia. The NLA adapted the UÇK designation from the Kosovo Liberation Army (*Ushtria Çlirimtare e Kosovës*) and retitled its organization *Ushtria Çlirimtare Kombëtare.* Thus, UÇK and NLA are synonymous.

4. Interview with Dr. Biljana Vankovska by Helen Tseresole, in the daily *Avghi* [Dawn], Athens, Greece, 9 May 2001. A copy of the interview was sent to the authors via e-mail from Dr. Vankovska in May 2001.

5. Ami Boué, *La Turquie d'Europe,* 4 vols. (Paris: A. Bertrand, 1840).

6. *Balkans,* from the Turkish, literally means "mountains." According to Zeune, "In the north this Balkan Peninsula is divided from the rest of Europe by the long mountain chain of the Balkans, or the former Albanus, Scardus, Hæmus, which, to the northwest joins the Alps in the small Istrian peninsula, and to the east fades away into the Black Sea in two branches." *Goea: Versuch einer wissenschaftlichen Erdbeschreibung* (Berlin, 1811), 11, quoted in Predrag Simić, "Do the Balkans Exist?" *The Southern Balkans: Perspectives from the Region,* ed. Dimitris Triantaphyllou, *Chaillot Papers* 46 (Paris: European Institute for Security Studies, 2001), 20.

7. For background on Czar Samuil, see the concluding paragraph of the section titled "Serbia" in "The Last Best Hope."

8. Stoyan Pribichevich, *Macedonia: Its People and History* (University Park and London: The Pennsylvania University Press, 1982), 95.

9. Alice Ackerman, *Making Peace Prevail: Preventing Violent Conflict in Macedonia* (Syracuse: Syracuse University Press, 1999), 54. Worthwhile discussion concerning religious toleration and the general lack of Ottoman proselytizing is from Pribichevich, *Macedonia*, 99. Janissaries were specifically recruited from the Ottoman non-Muslim population. See Pribichevich, *Macedonia*, 96–97 for details.

10. Pribichevich, *Macedonia*, 99–100.

11. Ackerman, *Making Peace Prevail*, 54.

12. Ibid.

13. John Shea, *Macedonia and Greece: The Struggle to Define a New Balkan Nation* (Jefferson, NC: McFarland and Company, 1997), 166.

14. Ibid., 169; 171.

15. Keith Brown, interview at the Watson Institute for International Studies, Brown University, 4 April 2001.

16. This geographic division is, admittedly, a contentious claim. In the interest of space and time, the above divisions reflect only the facts of *physical* geography of the region known throughout history as "Macedonia." The authors allow that the present Republic of Macedonia today comprises only a portion of what the Macedonian kingdom of Philip and Alexander represents. Further, the northwest and sections of the western region of the Republic of Macedonia, an area that is predominantly ethnic Albanian, themselves lie outside what is commonly considered the boundaries of ancient Macedonia. As an example of how boundaries in southeast Europe have become a geographical palimpsest, the villages of Debar, Kičevo, and Tetovo in Macedonia were part of the Kosovo "frontier" from 1913–1944.

17. Ackerman, *Making Peace Prevail*, 55.

18. Aydin Babuna, "The Albanians of Kosovo and Macedonia: Ethnic Identity Superceding Religion," *Nationalities Papers* 28, no. 1 (March 2000): 68.

19. Ibid.

20. Ibid.

21. Erich Frankland, "Struggling with Collective Security and Recognition in Europe: The Case of Macedonia," *European Security* 4, no. 2 (Summer 1995): 366.

22. *Kosova* (pronounced ko-SO-va) is the Albanian pronunciation of the area Serbs refer to as Kosovo-Metohija. *Kosovo* itself derives from the genitive form of the Serbian word for "crow"—referring to the defeat of Serbian medieval knights by Ottoman forces at *Kosovo Polje* (the "Field of the Black Birds") in 1389.

23. Jeffrey Smith, "Birth of New Rebel Army: Macedonian Guerilla Group Forming in Kosovo Poses Threat of Expanded Conflict in Balkans," *Washington Post,* March 30, 2001, A1. http//infoweb5.newsbank.com.

24. "War in the Balkans Again?" *Economist* 24 (March 30 2001): 57–58.

25. Notably, the document admitted that there are no military solutions to the problems in Macedonia and that any solution should be based on the "domestic political process intermediated by [*sic*] USA and EU." The document also focuses on three demands: rehabilitation and complete reintegration into society of NLA members; reconstruction of villages and family economies destroyed during the 2001 conflict, and allowing those citizens fulfilling their military [conscript] obligation to serve in their birth municipalities.

26. Loring M. Danforth, *The Macedonian Conflict: Ethnic Nationalism in a Transnational World* (Princeton: Princeton University Press, 1995), 142–43.

27. "Macedonia Constitution." Downloaded 18 April 2001 at http//www.uniwuerzburg.de/law/mk00000_.html.

28. Ivanov, 1; 3. Note that the terms *ethnic Macedonians, Slavs,* and *Macedonians,* are used interchangeably in the literature.

29. Shea, *Macedonia and Greece,* 242.

30. "Macedonia, The Former Yugoslav Republic of," *CIA World Fact Book 2000.* http://www.odci.gov/cia/ publications/factbook/geos/mk.html. The ethnic Albanian estimate is from Babuna, "Albanians of Kosovo," 81.

31. *1999 Country Reports on Human Rights Practices: Former Yugoslav Republic of Macedonia,* U.S. Department of State, 1–16. http://www.state.gov/www/global/human_rights/1999_hrp_report/macedonia.html.

32. Although their usage is problematic, the terms *ethnic Macedonians, Slavs,* and *Macedonians* are used interchangeably in the literature. This usage and understanding are indicative of the ill ease that exists in terms of ethnic identity within Macedonia, and we note that these terms will remain markers of difference as long as the synecdoche of "Macedonian" prevails over the sense that both Albanians and Slavs might reasonably associate with this identity.

33. To be accurate, we should acknowledge that the PDP represents both ethnic Albanian and Turkish constituencies.

34. Xhaferi allegedly suffered from Parkinson's disease and his health was deteriorating. For the sake of simplicity in what can only be termed a convoluted process, Xhaferi's party is referred to here as the DPA (the Democratic Party of the Albanians), despite the fact that party rulership and legal complications prevent its official registration with this designation; instead, Xhaferi's party is termed the PDP-A (Party for the Democratic

Prosperity of Albanians) and in 1999 held eight ministerial posts with eleven members of parliament.

35. IMRO's actual title is VMRO-Democratic Party for National Unity, from the Macedonian *Vnatreshna Makedonska Revolutsionna Organizatsiya,* and is one of a number of political parties to have appropriated the VMRO designation for its identity. (VMRO-Fatherland, VMRO-United, and the VMRO-Goce Delchev-Radical Democratic Party are three other examples.) All such organizations claimed that their existence was a continuation of the original Macedonian Revolutionary Organization created in 1893 and based in Thessaloniki, Greece. For simplicity, the term IMRO is used here rather than the more bulky yet correct marker of VMRO/DPMNE or IMRO/DPMNU. On parallel institutions, see Babuna, 81–82.

36. Mike O'Connor, "Slavs and Albanians Form Unusual Coalition in Macedonia," *New York Times,* November 30, 1998, A5.

37. Ibid., 6.

38. Gligorov, a former finance minister of the Socialist Federal Republics of Yugoslavia, and for decades a close associate of Tito's, earned the nickname of "the fox" for his political acumen, insight, and diplomatic skills. As president of the fledgling Republic of Macedonia, he helped establish the independent nation of Macedonia, successfully negotiated the withdrawal of the Yugoslav Army from Macedonia in 1992, and served as its only president until voluntarily retiring from public life in September 1999.

39. Ackerman, *Making Peace Prevail,* 57.

40. Ibid., 57–58.

41. Shea, *Macedonia and Greece,* 236.

42. Ackerman, *Making Peace Prevail,* 66.

43. Ibid., 67.

44. Ibid., 94.

45. Ibid., 93.

46. According to the international observers of Macedonia's elections, the elections were "marginally more transparent than previous ones" because a repeat vote occurred as a way to address inconsistencies. Still, more Slav Macedonians (33 percent to 65 percent) believed that the elections were fair than ethnic Albanians (59 percent to 32 percent). See "Opposition SDSM Pulls Ahead in FYROM," *Opinion Analysis,* Office of Research, Department of State, April 21, 2000.

47. Not surprisingly, Gligorov's personality and leadership seems to be the basis of this differentiation. Trajkovski was in some ways cursed by a quasi-legendary Macedonian "George Washington" who had preceded him as president.

48. "Macedonian Albanians' Political Influence Gives Them Reason for Optimism: But May Feed Suspicion among Ethnic Macedonians," *Opinion Analysis,* Office of Research, Department of State, May 9, 2000.

49. "Public Says Ailing FYROM Economy Needs Trade and Invest-ment for Growth," *Opinion Analysis,* Office of Research, Department of State, May 4, 2000.

50. "Opposition SDSM Pulls Ahead in FYROM," *Opinion Analysis.*

51. "Europe: Oh No, Not War in Macedonia as Well," *Economist* 10 (March 16, 2001): 46–47.

52. "Macedonia: Passing Clouds?" *Economist* 3 (March 9, 2001): 49.

53. Steven Erlanger, "Use Words, Not Guns, Balkan Leader Tells Rebels," *New York Times,* March 28, 2001, A4. The demand for the cen-sus and change in the preamble is from Steven Erlanger, "Wide Offensive by Macedonia Presses Rebels," *New York Times,* March 26, 2001, A1.

54. Ibid. The referenced quotations are found on A10.

55. Greece's objection to the very existence of Macedonia is well known. Originally dismissed as a "Tito-ist creation" and referred to in Greek as a *kratithio*—or statelet—Greece withheld recognition of the new state's designation as the Republic of Macedonia. Greece based its non-recognition policy on three points: (1) the kindred community of Macedo-nians and historical Macedonian regions that extended into Greece (known among Slavs as Aegean Macedonia) could foster future expansionist desires of the new state; (2) the name Macedonia clearly belongs to Greece and to Hellenic heritage; and (3) Greece objected to the new state's flag that depicted the Star of Vergina, a symbol that ancient Macedonians used, including Philip and Alexander, and to the new state's original currency that depicted the White Tower, a symbol of the Greek city of Thessaloniki (or Solon, in Macedonian). Greece not only tried to influence EU members to follow suit, but it also imposed an oil and commodity embargo, not includ-ing food and medicine, on the new state. Yet among Greeks—the most pragmatic and prosperous of all Balkan peoples—there was an incentive that appeared to be a compelling attraction in the tiny statelet to the north: economic profit. Despite Greece's intransigence on the issue of the name *Macedonia,* Greek businesses rapidly established commercial relations. In some ways, Greece came to secure Macedonia as an economic protectorate. Employing its Balkan prominence as EU and NATO member to establish business and trade with its neighbor to the north, for Greece the prospect of doing business in a stable Macedonia seemed too tempting to resist. By the year 2000, Greek (and Serbian) irredentist claims against Macedonia only a few years previous had effectively been muted by other realities.

56. Shea, *Macedonia and Greece,* 217–219.

57. Simić, 24.

58. Ibid., 28, fn. 31.

59. What the stability pact offered various Balkan nations was yet another incentive program for foreign investment. The U.S. contribution, which amounted to a $700 million aid, trade, and incentive program, included, for example, a $150 million fund to lure investors to the region,

a pledge of $130 million in support of small and medium-sized businesses, and a program of tariff reductions. Under its original charter, all the nations bordering Yugoslavia were slated to receive assistance; even within Yugoslavia, Montenegro was deemed eligible for direct assistance, although U.S. officials did not elaborate on how this could be achieved if Montenegro chose to remain a Yugoslav federal republic. According to the International Monetary Fund, Montenegro, Kosovo, Albania, Macedonia, Bulgaria, and Romania would require as much as $1.25 billion to $2.25 billion a year for the next several years in order to reasonably weather the enormous costs of trade disruption, refugee flows, and regional instability.

60. Jose Meirelles Passos, "The New War for Contracts," *O Globo* [Rio de Janeiro], June 13, 1999. Reprinted in *World Press Review* (September 1999): 15. These states include Albania, Bulgaria, Croatia, Macedonia, and Romania. The $100 billion estimate suggests the necessary cost to allow these various states to reach preconflict conditions of stability and growth potential. Kosovo, notably, has had no functional economic base or viable infrastructure in recent history.

61. John Brademas, "Promoting Democracy and Reconciliation in Southeastern Europe," *Mediterranean Quarterly: A Journal of Global Issues* 12, no. 1 (Winter 2001): 51–52.

62. Gjorge Ivanov, "The Albanian Question in Macedonia: The Macedonian Perspective." Paper provided to the authors in December 2000.

63. Thomas M. Franck, "Tribe, Nation, World: Self-Identification in the Evolving International System," *Ethics and International Affairs* 11 (1997): 155.

64. Georg Wilhelm Friedrich Hegel, *Political Writings,* trans. T. M. Knox (Oxford: Oxford University Press, 1964).

65. William James Hersh, *Blinding the Cyclops: Thinking the End of Racism* (Privately printed, n.d.), 26.

66. Isaiah Berlin, *The Crooked Timber of Humanity: Chapters in the History of Ideas* (New York: Alfred A. Knopf, 1991), 85.

67. Ibid., 224.

68. "Macedonians Disillusioned by NATO Action in Kosovo: Albanians Still Support NATO and Feel Safer with Troops in FYROM," *Opinion Analysis,* Office of Research, Department of State, April 25, 2000.

69. "Macedonia: Stability Pact Coordinator on Prospects for Peace," *BBC Worldwide Monitoring,* March 19, 2001. Downloaded on May 1, 2001, http://infoweb5.newsbank.com.

70. "Macedonia: Passing Clouds?" 48. Leonard J. Cohen, "Post-Milosevic [sic] Serbia," *Current History* (March 2001): 100.

71. "Macedonia: Passing Clouds?" 49.

72. Admittedly, the road to EU membership is a long one. The pact confers the status of potential EU candidacy to the FYROM, with a transition period of ten years toward full EU membership. For Macedonia, the

Stabilization Association Agreement was concrete EU recognition of the nation's political and economic progress, especially in the areas of regional cooperation and respect of fundamental rights. "The EU and Southeastern Europe: On the Road to Europe: First Stabilisation and Association Agreement, Signed on 9 April 2001 with Former Republic of Yugoslavia," Europa. Downloaded on April 25, 2001 at http://europa.eu.int/comm/external_relations/see/news/memo01_127.htm. For a review of the applicant process, see "A Survey of EU Enlargement: Europe's Magnetic Attraction," *Economist* 19 (May 25, 2001): 3–4.

73. Carl Bildt, "A Second Chance in the Balkans," *Foreign Affairs* (January/February 2001): 154.

74. Susan Woodward and Benn Steil, "A European 'New Deal' for the Balkans," *Foreign Affairs* (November-December 1999): 97–98.

75. One of the authors recalls a conversation with a senior American foreign service officer in 1993, during which the officer claimed that American policy would not radically alter its policy toward Greece for the sake of "a mere two million people in Macedonia." In hindsight, these remarks are extraordinary. America, after all, *did* radically alter its policy in 1999 for the sake of two million Serbs and Albanians living in Kosovo.

Imagining Macedonia

It is not symbolic geography that creates politics, but rather the reverse. . . . "Europe" ends where politicians want it to end, and scholars should at least be aware of this and how one's research can and is being used.[1]

—*Maria Todorova*

Following the horrific events of 11 September 2001, the security dilemma of the former Yugoslavia virtually vanished before the eyes of many policymakers. Perhaps understandably, the United States and Europe felt compelled to divert resources away from the region and into their mutual struggle against global terrorism. Yet for over a decade, the Balkans presented the West with one of its greatest strategic and policy challenges; the prosecution and aftermath of four violent conflicts—including the first military intervention by NATO—consumed billions of dollars and involved exhaustive diplomatic and regional initiatives.

The Balkans no longer constitutes a primary foreign policy challenge; this does not mean, however, that the international community can afford to look in all directions other than southeast Europe. The region itself is in a period of difficult, painful transition and stands the chance of rapidly succumbing to transnational criminal influences and becoming a "black hole" of terrorism such as happened in Afghanistan, which became not a sponsor of terrorism but rather a terrorist-sponsored state. Even as halting progress toward representative government and institution building takes place in Croatia, Serbia, and Kosovo, internal corruption, black market activities, and illegal arms shipments threaten the stability of the region. When twenty-five dollars can buy anyone a real, not a counterfeit, passport, the area has increasingly become attractive to those who easily escape the notice of already overstretched internal security forces. Nowhere has this security dilemma entered a more crucial period than in Macedonia.

Much of this changed security environment, inevitably, has left Macedonia both scarred and distorted. Indeed, as Robert Hislope has noted, "The Macedonian state itself encompasses a thoroughly corrupt set of institutions that has stymied democratic development, alienated ordinary citizens, and delegitimized the idea of an ethnically neutral, citizen-based, liberal state, especially among Albanians."[2] Given these negative outcomes, it seems worth remembering what Samuel Huntington emphasized in *Political Order in Changing Societies:* Corruption provides a means to assimilate new groups and new influences into a structured system.[3] Macedonia is a perfect example of an assimilating system, transitioning from the Socialist *apparatchik* of Yugoslavia to a state struggling with the tenuous transition to democracy. Corruption in "moderate doses"—if one could live with such a euphemism—can help overcome static bureaucracy and actually act as an instrument of progress.

Moreover, it seems worth emphasizing, as Huntington did, that corruption is a less extreme form of alienation than violence: "He who corrupts a system's police officers is more likely to identify with the system than he who storms the system's police stations."[4] In Macedonia, corruption is so pervasive that it actually perversely supports the stability of the government. That said, it remains a security issue that such a porous region has the potential—especially if it becomes increasingly overlooked by external actors—to become a thriving cesspool of criminal activity; 70 to 90 percent of heroin seizures in Europe, for example, have transited either through Kosovo, Albania, or Macedonia.[5]

To be sure, given the election results of September 2002, the citizens of Macedonia were ready for change. As a result, the coalition government of so-called "national unity" that had weathered the storm of the 2001 insurgency was thrown out of office one year later. Whether or not Macedonia survives truly does depend on "external" forces and actors. Clearly, the solutions for all southeast Europe will prove problematic and at times seem overwhelming. Macedonia may represent the greatest challenge as well as the last best hope for the Balkans.

LONGING FOR THE SOUTH

In Konstantin Miladinov's nineteenth-century poem "*T'ga za jug*" (Longing for the South)—which is as much a national poem of Macedonian identity as any that exists—there is both a wistful nostalgia for a landscape and a place that constitute a virtual heaven on earth. (Indeed, a translation into English of one of the poem's final lines reads: "The divine is everywhere.") Such admitted naïveté also has an immense attraction. In a real sense, all Macedonians—and here we must emphasize we mean all citizens of the Republic of Macedonia, be they Roma, Albanian, Turk, or Slav—take great pride in their achievements but also recognize the "false promise" of Macedonia as paradise on earth. Macedonia, to be blunt, if it is ever to be successful, still has a long way to go.

It was in recognition of this dichotomy between idealism and reality that the authors again visited Macedonia in August and (P. H. Liotta, again) in December of 2002. During the intervening months, during which we completed interviews with President Trajkovski (Appendix B), and members of the National Security Council as well as with representatives of the Organization for Security and Cooperation in Europe and the European Union, the republic underwent significant changes.

In terms of images and identities, we were physically struck while travelling through western Macedonia (in regions that were part of Kosovo during various periods in the twentieth century) in late August 2002 by how much political freedom and openness was accorded to all groups in the process leading up to the September elections. While many Slavs resented the context of the Ohrid

Framework Agreement, it seemed clear that Albanians took great pride in their political campaigns. Passing through Debar to the monastery of Sveti Jovan Bigorski, for example, we were fortunate enough to attend competing rallies of the Albanian PDK and DPA parties (which took place on competing ends of the town square).

We were immediately struck at seeing literally hundreds of vehicles—mostly vans and pickup trucks—flood down from the mountains to attend rallies in Debar. Each and every vehicle flew an Albanian flag from its roof or window, turning the landscape red with the outline of the black Albanian eagle. A year previous, displaying such pride in the Albanian nation within Macedonia would have landed someone in jail. Clearly, things had changed. Just as clearly, however, it seemed disturbing that of all the various campaign posters we saw of Albanian political parties, there were displays of the Albanian flag, the United States flag, and the flag of the European Union—but not one campaign poster displayed the flag of the Republic of Macedonia.

Thus, while the Ohrid Framework Agreement ostensibly brought peace to the region, it seemed clear that not everything had settled peaceably into place. The government coalition that "led" Macedonia through the KLA (National Liberation Army of Macedonia) insurrection of 2001 was voted out of office in September and replaced by a tenuous and untested coalition of Branko Crvenkovski's SDSM (Social Democratic Party) and Ali Ahmeti's Albanian DUI (Democratic Union of Integration). Notably, Ahmeti was the leader of the KLA insurrection in 2001 and proved himself a volatile subject in Macedonian politics.

Although the former government proclaimed the elections of September "the most successful in Macedonia's history," many private citizens considered the election to be a complete rejection of European and U.S. brokered efforts to implement peace and stability in the region. Specifically, many citizens viewed the Ohrid Framework Agreement of August 2001, which nominally symbolized the cessation of hostilities between ethnic Albanians and Slav Macedonians, with a general level of distrust—if not disgust. Slavs, in particular, seemed bitter toward the United States and its war against terrorism, because, rightly or wrongly, they believed the United States and the EU helped Ahmeti (whom many still regarded as a "terrorist") both receive general amnesty and secure a position of political authority in the government. Thus, rightly or wrongly, the perception among some was that violent means best secure political ends—whether in Kosovo or in Macedonia.

The seemingly peaceful conditions today in Macedonia belie a complex dynamic that can lead to future, possibly severe, conflict. Aside from the insurrection of 2001, a number of other events emphasized Macedonia's perceived marginalization. Although few, if any, actually expected to be offered membership in NATO at the Prague Summit in November 2002, almost all we spoke with believed that Macedonia had kowtowed to the West in order to curry favor and support, often at the expense of Macedonia's national identity. Several colleagues expressed their disappointment, for example, when President Trajkovski opted to attend a EU meeting in Malta rather than be present in Macedonia for Ilinden Day (which is the equivalent of the United States' Fourth of July). Indeed, Trajkovski was often seen by many citizens we spoke with as far too compliant with major power leaders and was largely perceived to lack the acumen and skill of his predecessor in office, Kiro Gligorov (who was Marshal Tito's finance minister and trusted friend for years in Socialist Yugoslavia). That said, one of the authors was shocked when a senior official referred to President Trajkovski in private conversation as the "Forrest Gump of the Balkans."

Such, unfortunately, are the political vagaries of Macedonia. In a region that has never been short of sorrow, Macedonia's many ironies and contradictions reached a tragic critical mass on February 26, 2004. On that day, an official delegation was in Ireland intending to present Macedonia's formal application for membership in the European Union. That delegation was withdrawn, and did not submit membership application, when news arrived that President Trajkovski's Super King Air 200 twin-engine turboprop had crashed near Mostar in Bosnia-Herzegovina. Six members of his official staff, along with the two pilots, also died.

The crash ended what was a relatively brief political career: Born in the village of Monospitovo near Strumica in southeast Macedonia in 1956, he received his law degree in Skopje in 1980. In December 1998, he was appointed deputy foreign minister by then-Prime Minister Ljupčo Georgievski—and continued in that position during the NATO-led intervention over Kosovo. Only one year later, on 15 December 1999, Trajkovski was sworn in as president of the Republic of Macedonia. Notably, Trajkovski had also studied theology in the United States, where he converted from the Macedonian Orthodox to the Methodist faith, and became a minister.

On the day of his death, Trajkosvki was on his way to attend an international conference on investment in the Balkans. Although rumors initially circulated that S-FOR French air traffic controllers might have had some part in the tragic accident, the greatest contributing factor was poor weather conditions.[6] Rain, cloud cover, and thick fog in the region had already forced Albania's prime minister, Fatos Nano, to cancel his own flight to the conference.

Clearly, Trajkovksi stirred up emotions in Macedonians, emotions sometimes complex and most often visceral. Writing in *Utrinski Vesnik* (The Morning Herald), Macedonia's second largest daily newspaper, Sonja Kramarska argued: "The more his fame grew on the international political scene, the more he sank into the clay of the Macedonian provinces . . . the Macedonian political elite was not prepared to admit to its ranks a conservative who began his career in Monospitovo and ended up praying in the White House [at the annual prayer breakfasts]."[7] Such brutal commentary, as the authors themselves observed, did not belie the attitude of many Macedonians we spoke with during the time of his public service.

Equally—and we wish to stress this—Trajkovski earned the reputation for honesty, and service, someone free of corruption. Although his Methodist faith was an exception to the predominant Orthodox and Muslim faiths predominant in the region, his faith also seemed to serve him as a guide, perhaps proving fundamental to his own vision of tolerance and reconciliation in a region most often torn by sectarian division and ethnic strife. He often ended his speeches with the words, "God Bless Macedonia." And, as one foreign diplomat with long experience in the region, put it: "Boris was fundamentally a good and honest man, which is not all that common among Balkan politicians."

Trajkovski also distinguished himself by *not* casting aside his professed positions during times of crisis. Unlike both former Prime Minister Georgievski and Albanian political leader Xhaferi, both of whom showed less resilient and integrative political positions in 2001 and after (when conflict came to Macedonia) than they did in 1999 (when the conflict was in Kosovo).[8] Indeed, during the 2001 crisis in Macedonia, Trajkovski relied heavily on his connections with the U.S. and the EU to help mediate the tensions that could have led to all-out war. Conversely, hard-liners in the VMRO-DPMNE, including Georgievski and hawkish Interior Minister Ljube Boskovski, clearly favored a military solution. Branko Trčkovski, in writing his obituary for Trajkovski in *Utrinski Vesnik,* offered: "You might remember that [Trajkovski] was the politician who kept constructive relations to Europe and the [United States] alive during the dramatic moments, when his . . . patron . . . Georgievski burnt all the bridges to the important centers in Europe and the world."[9]

In 2003, the authors also met privately with a number of senior and midlevel European representatives. Notably, and unlike most American diplomats, some of these individuals were fluent in Albanian, Macedonian, and Serbian and as much "expert" in the region as anyone can claim to be in the Balkans. (Further, it struck us that European diplomacy and political stability efforts have, to date, been generally far more successful and accomplished in Macedonia than have similar American efforts.) As a result of these extended conversations, we learned several disheartening facts. Although several details can never be written down as research product because of the implications it would have for Macedonia's national security, we did confirm a number of issues we have been studying over the past years. Most significantly, the widely held belief (which Western media promulgated) that the insurrection of 2001 was an ethnic conflict between Slavs and Albanians—just as Kosovo had been a conflict between Serbs and Albanians—was a distortion; to the contrary, the conflict of 2001 in Macedonia was as much an *intra-Albanian* struggle as anything else. This power struggle led to strange alliances as well: there is sound evidence, for example, that a hostage crisis in western Macedonia, which took place just prior to the September elections, was indeed a "staged" event with the knowledge and participation of both the (former) Slav Macedonian and ethnic Albanian political parties within the governing coalition.

Some we spoke with also expressed true skepticism about the abilities of the Albanian DUI party to successfully work with the Slav SDSM in a governing coalition. The DUI party, in particular, seemed to possess little or no political skill (or interest) other than that held by the highest leadership positions. We would note, however, that power politics—not ethnic division or manipulation—has always held the day in the previous brief history of Macedonia; there is no real reason to suspect it will not do so in the future.

One final troubling indicator of spillover effect, however, became manifest in the spring of 2003. A number of splinter insurgency groups from the Macedonian NLA (which was itself a "spillover" of the liberation armies of Preševo and the KLA of Kosovo) threatened to disrupt Macedonia's fragile peace. One group calling itself the "Albanian National Army" promised a "hot spring offensive" in 2003.[10] Publicly decrying the terms of the Ohrid Framework Agreement as "harmful and treacherous," the group vowed to attempt to create a "liberated" civil society—even if that meant at the point of a gun.

Perhaps ironically, the leader who received the most criticism from this group was Ali Ahmeti, the leader of the Macedonian NLA insurrection in 2001 and subsequent leader of the Albanian Democratic Union for Integration (DUI). (In the 2003 coalition, the DUI held five ministries in the center-left government of Branko Crvenkovski). Ahmeti, according to some, simply betrayed the very cause he led to "liberate" claimed injustices against Albanians for mere political convenience. In the words of one ANA member, "When I joined the [Macedonian] NLA [in 2001], I didn't fight for someone to take office and then form a brotherhood with the Slavs. When we were fighting, the leadership of the NLA claimed we were fighting against the Macedonian Slavs but now Ali Ahmeti want [sic] his son to be a friend of Jovan from Štip."[11]

THE END OF THE BEGINNING?

Macedonia's situation mirrors Great Britain's uncertain destiny when Winston Churchill declared in his nation's darkest hour: "We are not at the end, or the beginning of the end, but perhaps at the end of the beginning." Macedonia's fate, at this moment, truly hangs in the balance.

There is a pressing need to be specific and blunt about the fate of Macedonia. If the "international community"—admitting that the term itself is worthy of lengthy separate debate—supports the legitimacy of Macedonia as a state, then there is a direct responsibility to more firmly anchor that state's future. If the major players who will most affect the outcomes in the Balkan region cannot find some means of mutual accommodation and agreed to strategy, then the entire future European security architecture will be in peril. This accommodation must rest on valid and enduring principles as well as on the willingness of sustained commitment. This commitment must extend far beyond the small-scale intervention of Operation Essential Harvest that took place in September 2001 and must endure long after the principles of the Ohrid Framework Agreement (Appendix D).

While pessimistic assessments suggest that in 2001 in Macedonia we witnessed the end of the first decade of a new Thirty Years War, the true choice—for those who honestly believe in the notions of democracy, civil society, economic integration, and common security—seemed clear. Out of the immense complexities and new realities that Western intervention engendered by direct intervention in the Balkans, we can be sure of only one thing: The fate of Macedonia is up in the air. Institutions, alliances, and actors *can* affect a positive outcome.

In the end, it should not be so difficult to "imagine" Macedonia just as Maria Todorova "imagined" the Balkans in her brilliant assessment: we should view a place as it is—neither with positive nor negative valences—but as a landscape of possibility.[12] This is the real challenge of the future. At best, Macedonia will begin its slow progress—as will all the nation-states of the former Yugoslavia—to enter the fold of Europe. At worst, Macedonia will remain a place of otherness, a place that, as a prominent news analyst remarked to one of the authors privately, "Nobody cares about . . . unless there is blood being spilled."

To be sure, it is the citizens of Macedonia who will suffer most during this painful process of transition. Whether or not Macedonians will eventually enter Europe, or simply continue to be viewed as though some irredeemable mutant, cannot be answered by the Macedonians themselves.

To best conclude this imagining of Macedonia, then, we offer up a single image—related to the authors by the special representative of the European Union during the 2001 crisis. While evident that the real danger in 2001 was not the NLA insurgency, but rather the virus of hate which had the potential to infect whole communities and turn neighbors into monsters as well as victims, any number of Macedonians— Albanians and Slavs—struggled valiantly against the contamination.

Some, of course, proved more resistant than others. Perhaps none proved more resilient than the one man the senior diplomat passed by one day—who stood in the middle of a field in the heart of the heart of the conflict zone, stark naked, and strumming a guitar. In retrospect, he probably showed better perspective than anyone.

NOTES

1. Maria Nikolaeva Todorova, *Imagining the Balkans* (New York: Oxford University Press, 1997), 160; 139.

2. Robert Hislope, "Organized Crime in a Disorganized State: How Corruption Contributed to Macedonia's Mini-War," *Problems of Post-Communism* 49, no. 3 (May/June 2002): 33.

3. Samuel P. Huntington, *Political Order in Changing Societies* (New Haven: Yale University Press, 1968).

4. Quoted in Robert D. Kaplan, "Looking the World in the Eye," *Atlantic Monthly* (December 2001): 78.

5. Hislope, "Organized Crime," 34.

6. For reference regarding these rumors and the S-FOR air traffic controllers, see: March 2, 2004 edition of the daily press briefing of the French Ministry of Foreign Affairs. http://www.diplomatie.gouv.fr

7. *RFE/RL Balkan Report* [Radio Free Europe/Radio Liberty], Vol. 8, No. 9, March 5, 2004, compiled by Patrick Moore, "Macedonia: The Tragic End of an Honest President," Ulrich Buechsenschuetz (ub@itinerarium.de). http://www.rferl.org/reports/balkan-report/

8. For a review of their earlier 1999 positions, see pp. 14-17 of this text.

9. Quoted in *RFE/RL Balkan Report,* March 5, 2004.

10. The number of so-called "liberation armies" in the region can soon seem bewildering, but the Albanian National Army is often known as either the ANA or the AKSH—as part of the FBKSH (Front for the Liberation of Albania). Samples of the group's declarations, in Albanian and English, can be found at either htttp://www.shqiperiaebashkuar.com or http://www.freewebz.com/shqiperia. See also: Institute for War and Peace Reporting, *Balkan Crisis Report,* No. 403, Part I, 3 February 2003. <http:/www.iwpr.net>

11. *Balkan Crisis Report,* No. 403, Part I, February 3, 2003.

12. *Imagining the Balkans* (New York: Oxford University Press, 1997).

An Interview with Kiro Gligorov, First President of the Republic of Macedonia

The following interview took place at Villa Biljana on the shores of Lake Ohrid, Macedonia on 28 August 1999. P. H. Liotta, the researcher, helped shape the questions that were presented to President Gligorov during the interview. The journalist Richard Harteis conducted the interview. No part of this interview may be quoted from or referenced without the permission of P. H. Liotta or Richard Harteis.

President Gligorov had agreed to be interviewed at Tito's former summer palace, Villa Biljana. A former finance minister of the Socialist Federal Republics of Yugoslavia (SFRY), and for decades a close associate of Tito's, Gligorov earned the nickname "the fox" for his political acumen, insight, and diplomatic skills. As President of the fledgling Republic of Macedonia, he helped establish the independent nation of Macedonia, successfully negotiated the withdrawal of the Yugoslav Army from Macedonia in 1992, and served as its only president until voluntarily retiring from public life in September 1999.

At age 83, about to retire from politics, his thoughts on the significance of how his country had fared since declaring independence in 1991 were particularly valuable—especially given his country's pivotal role in the recent Kosovo crisis. President Clinton had thanked the Macedonian people earlier in the summer for welcoming

NATO troops and the 300,000 Kosovar refugees that poured into this small, Swiss-like country: "You bore this burden at great cost and considerable risk so that we could together pursue a vision of southeastern Europe very different from what the horrible ethnic cleansing in Bosnia and Kosovo represent."

Macedonia, the last multiethnic state that remained of the former Yugoslavia, had the potential to become the next Kosovo, with potentially hostile neighbors at its borders, and restless ethnic minorities within. Presidential elections took place in October 1999, with Boris Trajkovski chosen as the new president. With Gligorov gone, however, everything was up in the air.

Despite the loss of one eye and permanent shrapnel fragments in his head from an assassination attempt on 3 October 1995, in which 20 kilograms of explosive detonated in a car next to his, Gligorov remained in office until 1999.

Harteis: President Gligorov, you are the founding father of Macedonia, its George Washington, if you will, for American readers. You have kept Macedonia a safe island in troubled seas, and in 1995 even survived an assassination attempt on your own life.

As you prepare to leave the Presidency, can you tell me please what you consider your legacy may be for future generations? That is, what achievements are you most proud of and what regrets may you have?

President Gligorov: Your comparing me with George Washington is a little too daring (LAUGHTER). To understand how Macedonia avoided all the conflicts, the wars in Yugoslavia, to understand why, how she managed to do so, one must know Macedonian history. Except for the Second World War when we fought against the fascist front, organizing our own army, and liberating Macedonia, in all other uprisings or wars, we have always been the loser. We have always lost the battle. For instance, we celebrate the Ilinden uprising of 1903 as our national day. In fact, this was a very big tragedy for our nation. We had a republic for ten days in Kruševo. And afterward a great [Ottoman] army carried out massacres, burnings, and deportations. This is when the great Macedonian exodus began to Bulgaria and other countries. And this exodus continued for a very long period of time. This is why our people feel that they want nothing to do with war.

I understood this. I knew this, and when the separation from the former Yugoslavia occurred, I declared publicly to all television media and in the assembly, that Macedonia could survive only if it remained with its existing borders. Why did I stress this? It was because for the last hundred and twenty years, for part of the nineteenth century and throughout the twentieth, there have been continuous wars from neighboring countries trying to conquer Macedonian territory. In 1913 a tragic event occurred with the Bucharest Treaty which divided Macedonia into parts. The biggest part of the territory of Macedonia went to Greece. Thirty-eight percent, that is the actual size of our present state, went to what became Yugoslavia.

The remaining part was divided between Albania and Bulgaria. So, our people lived with this feeling that Macedonians are divided and they cannot live together even though they are the same geographic territories. Realizing this, and aware of the fact that none of our neighbors was ready to give up part of the territory or population, and trying to avoid any war or conflict or battles for Macedonia, I stressed this view at the time. And other people responsible in the state, to whom I said that I would do this publicly, told me it was a very dangerous thing to do, that it was against the wishes of the people.

Harteis: Insisting on existing borders?

Gligorov: Yes. And that that action would have dire consequences. Nevertheless, I declared this position publicly in front of the Assembly and on television, having in mind the fact that our people did not want war. And there was no reaction. Afterward, in order to convince all of our neighbors that we did not have any territorial aspirations, we wrote in our constitution that we do not have any territorial claims against any of our neighbors and that we do not wish to interfere with their internal affairs.

The only thing that we want is that these countries respect international standards for minority rights, and to provide that the country enjoys these rights. So this was crucial for Macedonia. By having this policy, our neighbors had no reason to attack Macedonia. Our second aim was to acquire our independence through peaceful and legitimate means. And this is how we did it. During the national referendum, the people voted by a high percentage for independence since this had been their wish for several generations in the past.

The third thing necessary to be truly independent was to make the Yugoslav army leave the country peacefully. We wrote into our constitution that no foreign army could remain in the country six months after the adoption of that constitution. During this period war had already broken out in Croatia—let me recall the destruction of Vukovar. And later the initial disputes in Bosnia began. There is still research to be done on why the Yugoslav authorities were willing to withdraw their armies peacefully.

Harteis: How that actually was achieved?

Gligorov: Yes. Why they agreed so easily. I would say that one of the reasons was perhaps because they were already at war with two of the former republics of Yugoslavia and they would need to open a third front if they wanted to enter into a conflict with Macedonia. That is when we began our discussions or negotiations with the headquarters of the Yugoslav army.

The first meeting we had was unsuccessful. They accused us of betraying our common country state. And it was obvious it would be difficult to reach an agreement in such an atmosphere. But the defense minister in charge at the time, General Veljko Kadijević, was soon replaced, and General Blagoje Adžić replaced him [in 1992] as commander-in-chief [and defense minister]. This was a soldier who had been in Macedonia for ten years, in several cities.

He called and said he wanted to come for a meeting. I told him he was always welcome. If his mission is to withdraw the army peacefully, then there is no problem. He came. We had very difficult talks. What's more, I made this decision without consulting with any other authorities in the country—all this was happening very fast. These talks lasted eight hours.

Instinctively, I understood that the issue was whether the army would be able or allowed to take all their equipment with them when they withdrew. And that's when I said to him, "I have a suggestion: If you leave Macedonia peacefully, then take all the weapons the army has. We do not intend to enter into war so we won't need any arms."

That's the point at which the talks changed, took another course. We agreed to establish three commissions with generals from both sides to make a list of everything that the army would be taking with it when it left. After about an hour, they came back with a very long list. That is when I first became aware of everything that the army had by way of equipment here in Macedonia. There were very large reserves. All kinds of weapons, very modern weapons, since the army that was stationed in Macedonia had the task of defending the southern border against NATO. They had enormous stores of fuel, oil, food, medicine, everything. Underground warehouses. And all this material was listed. I began to read the list, and immediately on the first page, I saw two items that must not be taken. The first problem was that all the radar from the Skopje and Ohrid airports were to be taken. This would mean that we would be completely isolated, that no one could enter Macedonia and no one could go anywhere. At that point, I told him we were ready to defend this with our lives because we could not survive as a state without an airport. I said he knew very well that all foreign currency reserves were in Belgrade and that we would be unable to purchase such equipment, and would, in any event need far too much time to do so.

The second thing I saw they wanted to take was all the drugs and medical supplies. These included reserves for a war lasting six months. And I told him no, that the military hospital in Skopje served not only the military staff. More than half of the patients there are civilians. And if you were to take all the instruments and all the medicines from this hospital, this would leave a very bad impression on the people of what you did, how you left the country. So, we talked about this matter a long time, for hours. And he said, "I understand all that you are saying, but the army that will be leaving Macedonia will need radar, its own airport where it is going as well as its own hospital." But at last we agreed that this was to remain. But nevertheless he told me that the most important and the biggest radar had already been taken to Belgrade the previous night. (LAUGHTER) And this was the radar that controlled altitudes greater than 4500 meters.

Harteis: How did you manage to convince him? Why did he relent?

Gligorov: It was not at all easy. I can even give you a bizarre detail. Two days before the general came, it had already been announced in the media that the commander-in-chief of the Yugoslavian army would be visiting Macedonia to discuss these issues. And there was a citizen who called me from Prilep, a city in Macedonia, and he said to me, "Do you know that I have been in the military academy with General Adžić from the very first day. And we are very good friends. We were roommates. I have a photo of him from that period of time," he said, and he asked me, "Would you allow me to come and meet with him?"

Not knowing how the talks would go, whether it would be appropriate, I told him, "Please send me the photo today, and afterwards I will inform you if it will be appropriate to come depending on the talks." Adžić was in Prilep too as a soldier, did his military service in Prilep.

During the talks, when there was a very hot issue being discussed, I showed him the photo and I asked him, "Do you know this man?"

"Yes I know him. He is Georgi from Prilep. He is my friend."

And he asked me, "How is he? I'd like to see him."

It was important that he changed.

Harteis: Because of the human contact?

Gligorov: Yes. He changed his behavior completely.

Harteis: The friends of one's youth are always very important.

Gligorov: So, after that the whole situation became more agreeable. He began to tell me about the many years he had served in Macedonia, that he found us to be a very fine and peaceful nation (LAUGHTER) and that he felt very good when serving here. Then he raised the proposal I was describing to you.

Harteis: That broke the ice?

Gligorov: Yes. They withdrew nonstop for forty-five days. Tanks, planes, all of it. Artillery, reserves, everything. And in order to prevent anything from happening, we gave them a continual security escort to accompany them to the border. And when we agreed, after the eight hours of talks, I said to them, "I don't know what you think, but I think we have done a very good job. Let's have lunch. And before that, let's have a cognac or two." (LAUGHTER) Then we had one, then two, then three cognacs. And the atmosphere completely changed. We accompanied them to the border with Yugoslavia. And in the evening we released a statement that we had concluded this agreement and that the army would be withdrawing peacefully.

Let me tell you about another small episode. It was evening and I was sitting in my office. One of my advisors entered and told me that members of one of the most nationalist parties in Macedonia had gone to the main barracks in Skopje, had surrounded this place, and were trying to take the equipment from it. I told my secretary to find the general secretary of the party and invite him to come to see me, that it was very urgent. I don't know how she managed to do it, but in fifteen minutes he was in my office.

And I immediately said to him as he entered the door, "If you don't give the order immediately to withdraw your party members and convince them to turn back, you will cause a huge tragedy and you will have to take the responsibility for the matter." At the time we didn't have any weapons. We had only a few hundred guns on the list. He listened to me, and he went immediately to the spot and he told them that the party had ordered the withdrawal.

Harteis: Now these arms were arms that had not been taken out by the Serbians?

Translator: No, this is an episode before the agreement.

Gligorov: I am telling you this, you see, because, if they wanted to, they could have arrested me, arrested the government, and two or three party leaders, and they could have finished the job. So, the occupation would have been short.

Harteis: So, another example of why Macedonia is lucky to have you.

Gligorov: No, let me say again: If I have any merit in all this, it is only to have understood and to have known the feelings of these people. Well, you see, we must turn to history once again. You see from here the old part of the town, you can see it very well from here [pointing to the far side of Lake Ohrid]. How were they able to find the right location for the town. If you try to build a house over there, if you try to set the foundations of your house, you will discover the ruins of Slavic civilization, the parts of the Ottoman Empire, then Roman, Greek, and so on, Byzantine.

Harteis: And even Orpheus lived in these mountains.

Glogorov: Yes, and despite the fact that we did not have the opportunity to go to school and learn our own language, we have inherited all these civilizations, they were passed down though our families, from parents to children. Perhaps you know that a citizen from Ohrid, Grigor Prličev, won the highest prize from the Athens University for his poem "Serdarot" (in Greek, "O Armatolos") which was written in Greek at that time. And this tradition still lives. We are a small country and we have a large number of poets. Maybe they aren't all the best, but some of them are recognized on a European and world level.

Harteis: One or two more quick questions. What do you believe Macedonia's future will be vis-à-vis, well, let me put it this way . . . the recent military actions by NATO in Kosovo have caused political and economic difficulties for Macedonia. But Macedonia has responded generously to the Kosovo refugees. Do you feel the NATO action was unavoidable, and to what degree would you support its continuing presence in the area if you were to continue as President after October. That is, what do you feel Macedonia's policy toward Kosovo should be?

Gligorov: From the beginning we supported the action of the European Union and NATO regarding the issue of Kosovo. The reason is very simple.

If the Kosovo crisis was not resolved the way it was, then it could have developed into a Balkan crisis and could have become a Balkan war. Since our orientation is to become a member of NATO and the European Union, we considered it a duty to support NATO and the European Union. First, we allowed the OSCE (Organization for Security and Cooperation in Europe) monitoring forces to enter Kosovo. And we allowed extraction forces to enter Macedonia that could get them out in case of danger. Afterward we allowed 14,000 NATO troops.

Harteis: So, you discussed with President Clinton that you were willing to have troops come to Macedonia but only on one condition, that they be restricted in their movements, to be defensive rather than any sort of aggressive.

Interpreter: They were going to Kosovo only in the case of a peace agreement being reached.

Harteis: As peace monitors?

Gligorov: And fortunately this is what happened.

Harteis: In the future then, how do you see Macedonia's relationship to Kosovo? Because it seems such a troubled sea again, I'm wondering if, well, for example, your relationship with Albania. It seems the Albanian government and the Albanian minority that you have here is somewhat the key to any potential future problem. How do you think any possible tensions can be diminished in terms of the so-called "larger Albania?"

Gligorov: The Greater Albania?

Harteis: (LAUGHTER) Yes. The Greater Albania. We know that the population here tends in Muslim families to expand in a bigger way, that they have a higher birth rate, and also that you have the refugees coming in from Kosovo. And suddenly your population was 50 percent Muslim and suddenly this delicate balance among minorities threatens to become—I don't want to prejudice you in your answer—but, how do you see the tensions being diminished in terms of keeping what is a very large part of your population actively involved in your government, at work and so forth. How are you defusing that potential problem?

Gligorov: You're right when you say that this is a potential problem. But I will explain the structure of the population. Two-thirds of the population is Macedonian. 22.9 percent are Albanian. 7 to 8 percent Turks, we have Romas (Gypsies), Serbs who are 2 percent, and Armenians who are a small minority. So in this direction we are more of a multicultural community. In this case, the Kosovo crisis, the Albanians organized several demonstrations that occurred in Tetovo, in Skopje.

Harteis: Regarding the university in Tetovo?

Interpreter: No, regarding the question of Kosovo.

Gligorov: These were peaceful demonstrations in which they showed their solidarity with their brothers in Kosovo. And we understood this. It would have been different if those demonstrations were violent, with the destruction of shops or houses and so on. This would not have been accepted. Why not?

First, we must keep two facts in mind. Even though Albania, Macedonia, and Bulgaria have weak economies, nevertheless, people live much better in Macedonia than in Kosovo and in Albania. And Albanians know this fact very well. They think about their families. And I think they would not want to be part of Greater Albania that would be led by Tirana. Because there was a regime over there for fifty years and now only two years ago the authorities were destroyed. The arms were all taken from the arsenals. And as a consequence there are a lot of gangs, weapons traffic, and drug traffic. Whereas in Macedonia, they live peacefully, and everyone is allowed to work. This is one reason.

The second reason is that Macedonia has never been at war with the Albanians. On the contrary, we have been in the same situation during the Ottoman Empire and the time of Yugoslavia. And we have fought together to have our own education, to have our own language, to have our own self-government. So, in the Second World War as well, we had joint Macedonian/Albanian units that fought against occupation. And the people who were in these units, some of them are still alive. And they know, and they can understand the difference between living in Macedonia and Kosovo and Albania.

Harteis: Your concern would not be from the ethnic Albanian population. My understanding is that they are trying to work peacefully in this country to resolve the questions, whether it be insufficient representation in the government by their definition, or maybe the universities not being accredited. It's not the Macedonian-Albanian population. If you have a healthy and happy population within Macedonia, then this threat from without will not be a realistic one.

Gligorov: Yes. The most important thing for us would be for Macedonia to be developed economically. And if we live better in Macedonia than in Serbia, Kosovo, Bulgaria, and Albania, then Albanians will remain here.

There is one more reason that is important. For decades there was an Albanian university in Priština. And in Macedonia, Albanians have enjoyed the right since 1944 to have elementary and secondary education exclusively in the Albanian language. They have their own media, their own newspapers, radio stations, TV stations. They have their own political parties. They participate in all parliamentary, local, and other elections. And they are a coalition partner in the government. Not just since the independence of Macedonia in 1991, but since the creation of the Republic of Macedonia in 1944. As a result of this, there is an intelligentsia both here and in Kosovo, and they believe that they are on a higher cultural level than is the case in Albania. And if some Greater Albania were ever to be established, then it would be very difficult for them to decide who would lead whom. So, it is one thing to talk about Albania as a goal, as an objective. But it is a completely different issue if such a state were actually to be created.

Harteis: But given your pacifistic nature here in Macedonia, this ideal— I think almost of a little Switzerland, peaceful, with other countries around and very successful. Given the fact that you eschew war, if you had a neighbor, be it Albania or any of your other neighbors who felt more aggressive toward you, do you see that as a possible risk, that some regime in the near future might try to incite the kind of ethnic unrest which was the case in some of these recent wars in the Balkans, do you see that as a problem? That is, an exterior threat, not the internal population. How would you confront that sort of threat on a political level?

Gligorov: There are always such threats in the Balkans. Not only the case of Macedonia. It is so in other states of the Balkans. The Balkans are very mixed. And there is no one nation [that is itself a] country. There are minorities everywhere. And the problem in the Balkans should not be how to take some territories from other countries, or to change borders.

Harteis: Our former Ambassador to Bulgaria, H. Kenneth Hill, said once that the Balkans has more history than it can consume.

Gligorov: Yes. (LAUGHTER)

Harteis: I think I am overstepping the bounds of courtesy by staying this long, but perhaps a final question. What are your future plans?

Gligorov: Well you see, I have thought about it already a year ago, whether to continue in this position or not—of course, that is if the people were to choose me to continue it. Or whether it is high time to leave this post to someone else, to someone younger. In May I entered my eighty-third year of life. (LAUGHTER)

Harteis: *Živi y zdrave!* [Life and Health]

Gliigorov: And the mandate of the president lasts for five years so this would mean I would be the same age as Tito when he died. And I know very well. I was a witness. Tito with his wisdom, his intelligence, his political instinct was a very healthy man. But the last ten years he did not have the necessary energy to achieve his ideas. And he was surrounded by people who were constantly bringing him news, inviting him, and so on. They even tried to divorce him from his wife. Something that he did not allow until his death. But, nevertheless, they did bring about a separation, making them live in separate houses.

And Tito began to interfere in the business of the republics, and these were not very good interventions. First, he changed the Croatian governing body, then the whole Serbian authority. And during that period, Serbia had the best government. These were young people who were educated abroad with a liberal orientation. Afterward, there was a complete change of the Macedonian authorities. Many misunderstandings and disputes among the republics arose. And there were also economic difficulties that occurred. Then the republics began to blame each other over the economic situation. This was a perfect breeding ground for nationalism and gave birth to the question of why people should be governed by someone else, why they should remain in this federation. It began first in Slovenia, then Croatia, Bosnia, and Macedonia.

Harteis: Do you still believe in some sort of federation for this part of the world? Or do you feel now that it's clear Macedonia must, as its constitution indicates, have its national borders? Do you see this as a permanent, independent state?

Gligorov: I think that after everything that happened in the territory of the former Yugoslavia, it is not very probable. So we could not insist on some kind of political association. But this does not mean that if we respect each of these countries as independent entities, there cannot be cooperation. It is obvious that after seventy years of common life, there are many friendly business and family ties that play a very important role. That is why the Macedonian population accepted very un-heartedly the strikes against Yugoslavia.

Harteis: But you feel that they were unavoidable, nevertheless.

Gligorov: Yes. The people didn't object because of some feeling for Serbia, but because everyone in Macedonia had someone, a friend or a relative, over there. And they were constantly concerned about those people.

Harteis: What do Macedonians think of Americans?

Gligorov: In all public opinion polls that were taken in Macedonia, and even during the air strikes against Serbia and Kosovo, a very large percentage of Macedonians were in favor first of all of Americans and then other nations followed. This feeling is real, it exists, even despite the fact that America, that the United States, did not support us vis-à-vis Greece concerning the dispute over the name of our country. Nevertheless, the United States helped us very much to strengthen our independence, to become members of international organizations. And they also made a great effort to support us economically and with technology.

Harteis: It's an unfortunate way of learning about a country. In America we are somewhat isolated. We have oceans between us. And the man in the street in America may not know where Macedonia is on the map. It is an unfortunate way to learn about a country to have a war, to follow the news, to see the refugees and so forth. But I think it safe to say, to say back to you that America has a very positive feeling for Macedonia. It was extremely moving to see this tragedy, to see the butchery taking place, and to see Macedonia's welcoming the refugees. It proves perhaps that living a politics of idealism has rewards. That it works. Because I think our two countries, or at least I hope that our two countries will continue to have very positive feelings about each other and come to know more about each other. Your giving me this much time today, sir, is perhaps going to help.

Gligorov: No, no, it was a great pleasure for me.

Appendix B

An Interview with Boris Trajkovski, Second President of the Republic of Macedonia

The following interview took place at Villa Biljana by the shores of Lake Ohrid, Macedonia from 22 to 24 August 2002. Notably, this interview lacked the informality and good humor of the interview with Kiro Gligorov, Trajkovski's predecessor as president, three years previous. All questions put to the president had to first be vetted through the National Security Council of Macedonia, and while none of the questions were challenged or modified, the responses are carefully scripted and lack the spontaneity of the Gligorov interview.

Boris Trajkovski was inaugurated as the second President of the Republic of Macedonia on December 15, 1999. (He died in office—killed, along with eight others, in a plane crash in Bosnia-Herzegovina on February 26, 2004.) Before assuming the presidency, he served as Deputy Minister of Foreign Affairs in the center-right government of Ljupčo Georgievski's Internal Macedonian Revolutionary Organization-Democratic Party of Macedonian National Unity (VMRO-DPMNE). Trajkovski, a lawyer by training, has the unusual distinction of being a Methodist pastor in a predominately Orthodox and Muslim country. He gave up communism and Orthodoxy while studying theology in the United States, returning to his homeland to join the ranks of Macedonia's small protestant community.

Although Trajkovski's pro-European and anti-Communist rhetoric resonated well with ethnic Slav and ethnic Albanian voters, Albanians were clearly the driving force behind Trajkovski's second-round runoff win against Tito Petkovski, the Social Democrat's presidential candidate and first-round victor. Trajkovski moderated his remarks about the demands of minority groups, and shortly before the second round of elections, Albanian leader Arben Xhaferi of the DPA called on his supporters to elect Trajkovski, effectively clinching his presidential bid. (DPA subsequently joined in the governing coalition with VMRO-DPMNE. Notably, Trajkovski later resigned his VMRO party membership, perhaps to maintain a sense of neutrality as president.)

The clashes between Macedonian forces and ethnic Albanian guerrillas in 2001 presented Trajkovski with numerous challenges. He appeared, nonetheless, to take great pride in the Ohrid Framework Agreement of 2001 and, despite the contrary views of some of his countrymen, believed that the agreement would lead to lasting peace between Slavs and Albanians in Macedonia.

Following the initial interview work with President Trajkovski in August, Stevo Pendarovski, National Security Advisor to the President of the Republic of Macedonia, helped coordinate a follow-up interview after the elections of 15 September 2002 (in which both VMRO-DPMNE and DPA were voted out of power). P. H. Liotta returned to Macedonia in December 2002 to complete the final series of interviews and conduct further study for this book. The researchers remain grateful that members of the National Security Council cooperated fully with our numerous requests for information.

All of the responses to these questions are the official response of President Trajkovski.

Liotta and Jebb: How do you see Macedonia one year after the Ohrid Framework Agreement?

Trajkovski: Generally speaking, the situation in the Republic of Macedonia one year after the Framework Agreement is much different now than in the same period last year. The reintegration of the formerly affected back into the constitutional order of the state is practically finished, and 90 percent of the displaced persons have already returned to their homes, which have been repaired with European Union funds. Finally, the government of the Republic of Macedonia and all citizens, regardless of their ethnic background, are now reoriented toward economic prosperity and well being—issues that were not even considered last year.

We have, of course, many challenges ahead of us, on security, economic, and political levels. We will face the major one very soon, with the elections of 15 September [2002], when the new parliament of the Republic of Macedonia will be constituted and a new government elected. It is imperative for the Republic of Macedonia to acquire a legal and legitimate government, which enjoys credibility among the majority of the people [and who believe] that it will pursue reforms headed in the direction of full integration with the Euro-Atlantic structure.

Liotta and Jebb: What should or could the United States and the European Union do for the Republic of Macedonia, or have they done too much?

Trajkovski: Many analysts who closely follow the situation in this part of Europe share the opinion that the United States and the EU had an exceptionally rapid, timely, and synchronized reaction to our crisis. It is true that without their support, which continued through the entire crisis, we would have been unable to prevent and later on reduce the negative consequences of the crisis. The signatures of the EU and United States representatives on the Framework Agreement gave an additional validity that none should underestimate.

Despite the fact that from time to time there are some persons who, on behalf of the United States appear, allegedly with good intentions to help Macedonia and, in fact, act in contradiction with such commitments, there are no arguments that can seriously put into doubt the positive role that the United States generally had in the course of last year's crisis.

Liotta and Jebb: Is the Republic of Macedonia still closely related to Kosovo or are their future and fate independent of each other?

Trajkovski: The security of the states in the region is a complex issue, and individual answers should not be given. Pushing the resolution of one issue in a region without taking into account the implications it could have on other parts is only a partial action. Good examples of this partial action include attempts to pacify the Preševo Valley in 2000. After the Yugoslav army, supported by NATO, entered the Ground Safety Zone (GSZ), a large number of former fighters of the UÇPMB transferred to Macedonia.

Therefore, in the region there are a considerable number of well-armed and well-trained extremists who—most often in order to protect their criminal interests or quasi-political platforms—produce conflicts in the countries of the region. These forces should be demilitarized and disbanded in an integral way. By doing this, the major threat to the region would be definitely eliminated.

Thus, in one respect, we can conclude that the stability and security of the Republic of Macedonia will very much depend on the development of democracy in the region, especially in Kosovo. Here we are talking about a common border of over 100 kilometres, which at the moment is not entirely closed to the illegal activities of criminal structures and paramilitaries with nationalist ideologies.

Liotta and Jebb: Do crime and corruption threaten the security in the region of southeast Europe?

Trajkovski: I guess that we are all aware that for a long time now the answer to that question is "Yes." The real question now is how to reduce its destructive effect on the development of democracy, stability of institutions, and the economic prosperity of states. Organized crime and corruption in this part of Europe have never been put under control, probably because current and former political elites have never had a clear political will to do that. It should be clear to us, however, that by giving organized criminal groups the chance to expand their influence and territory, this means placing the very foundations of the state in danger. These foundations, if not already, can fall under the full domination of criminalized and corrupted groups.

By doing this, the region will lose indispensable support from EU and NATO structures, since the dimensions of this regional phenomenon will exceed the capacity and potential that regional states have at their disposal to control this threat.

Liotta and Jebb: Which prejudice would you like to correct in relation to Macedonia? Which positive aspect would you single out?

Trajkovski: The sole act of the independence of the Republic of Macedonia was accompanied by a series of prejudices. These prejudices mainly focused on the opinion that Macedonia would not be able to survive as an independent, sovereign state, that Macedonia wouldn't last long, that it suffered from irresolvable problems—and similar other forecasts, drafted mainly by people who did not wish Macedonia well. But ten years of independence are the best proof for squelching these prejudices, for proving that they have been wrong. Not only did we survive as a sovereign, independent state, but the Republic of Macedonia, throughout this past decade, remained a pillar of stability, and a stabilizing process in this turbulent region. Until last year the Republic of Macedonia was not a consumer but a producer of peace. We received recognition from the entire international community for this achievement.

Last year, unfortunately, the Republic of Macedonia was exposed to a brutal attack from terrorist groups led by criminal incentives, whose ultimate goal was to provoke civil war in Macedonia that would result in the division of the country. The temptation proved major—and some of those scattered prejudices resurfaced, pushed by those who insisted they were right all along. Fortunately, for all the citizens of the Republic of Macedonia, this time they proved wrong once again. The Republic of Macedonia managed to efficiently and rapidly deal with the crisis, absorbing the crisis within institutional systems and processes and making Macedonia one of the most developed countries with respect to the treatment of ethnic communities and respect for national and human rights. This is the strongest positive impression I bear and I, as President, will never forget it, and neither will all the citizens of the Republic of Macedonia, who, even during the most difficult times last year preserved their dignity and their commitment to live together in peace, regardless of political, religious, or national background.

Therefore, once and for all, I want to remove the prejudice that Macedonia cannot develop as an independent, sovereign and stable state under the current constitutional order.

Another prejudice I would rectify is the prejudice that the Republic of Macedonia is situated in the Balkans, and that the Balkans must be treated as region that only creates problems and conflicts for Europe. I don't like it that when many people speak of the Balkans, the first thought they have is "war." I and all other leaders from the region must pursue intense political and diplomatic activity through regional and multilateral cooperation, to fully stabilize the region and to begin to achieve our identical visions in a concrete way—this means integration of our countries within European and Euro-Atlantic structures. Therefore, the Balkans are neither in Africa nor Asia so as to require some kind of rapprochement with Europe. The Balkans are part of the continent of Europe and will have to start to live in a European manner. The rest of Europe needs the Balkans just as the Balkans needs the rest of Europe.

Note: The following responses were provided following the elections of 15 September 2002.

Liotta and Jebb: What are your expectations from the international community—particularly from Europe and the U.S.A.—now that Macedonia has peacefully completed the successful elections of 15 September?

Trajkovski: We have already opened lines of communications with both the EU and the United States, and we must maintain and strengthen them in the near future. One first framework is the Stabilization and Association Agreement we signed with the EU in 2001. As a first country from the region to do this, and following the parliamentary elections, we are ready to return to all obligations and provisions from the agreement as an anteroom for gaining status as an aspirant state as soon as possible.

With NATO, we have had [a] long-standing partnership for a decade. In this last year, through two missions of the Alliance, we have had high levels of interoperability between our security forces and NATO soldiers, so our intention is to extend mutual cooperation into the next year. Under this changed role and a different mandate, we must shift toward civilian orientation rather than just peace keeping missions. This shift might help us shorten the road to full membership.

Thus, my expectations from Euro-Atlantic structures in the near future are that we will be judged, rightly so, by our level of democracy and contribution to regional stability. During the process of enlargement, we should not forget that we are the last successful multiethnic democracy in this part of Europe.

In this regard, I am deeply satisfied by the level of commitment and support offered to us by the United States, which although preoccupied and heavily engaged in many other regions in the world, consistently maintains high levels of cooperation with the Republic of Macedonia.

Liotta and Jebb: Were you surprised by the election results, particularly strong support for SDSM over VMRO?

Trajkovski: In the preelection period, several domestic and foreign agencies predicted similar outcomes, with the American IRI [International Republican Institute] having the most accurate overall estimate.* But, for me as president of this country, much more significant was the high turnout of more that 73 percent of the electorate as well the peaceful and democratic atmosphere in which the elections took place.

Liotta and Jebb: How differently do you expect to work with the new government than you did with the previous government? Will integration with the European Union and other multilateral frameworks receive the same emphasis as it had?

Trajkovski: At the very beginning of the election campaign, and just before election day, I delivered two addresses to the nation in which I emphasized the most important topics I would like to see on the agenda of the next government. While I stated clearly that I cooperate with and support every government, regardless of its constituent parties, we must do everything possible to fight poverty, organized crime, and corruption, and we must also provide for the territorial integrity and sovereignty of the country while equally securing a calm and safe environment for all citizens, regardless of their ethnicity. My foreign policy agenda is well known since 1999, and I will continue to push for full integration in the EU and NATO. This priority has been accepted by the winning coalition, and I am now waiting to see their operational platforms and hard work begin.

Liotta and Jebb: How would you respond to those who object to the legitimate victory of Ali Ahmeti's party Democratic Union for Integration (DUI) among Albanian voters? How do you reconcile the view of some Macedonians who regard Mr. Ahmeti as a "terrorist" because of his involvement with the events of 2001 in Macedonia, even though Mr. Ahmeti has repeatedly called for reconciliation and worked to implement the Ohrid Agreement?

Trajkovski: Everyone must respect the legitimate will of others and so it was shown when the last polls closed on election day. In order to have peace in the country, the former military parastructure was granted amnesty, and the reasons for that decision were broadly elaborated at the time. All these horrible scenes are behind us and now it is time to work for peace. This is one side of the conflict in Macedonia where political pragmatism obliges us to work for the happier future of the coming young generations. Saying this, I am not agitating at all for forgiveness and amnesia of what happened last year, but that side of the conflict has to be dealt with by the International Tribunal in Hague.

Liotta and Jebb: What lessons does Macedonia provide for other countries that are newly democratizing?

Trajkovski: In the last ten years we have passed through many difficulties, from embargoes to economic sanctions to disputes about our constitutional name to the air campaign against Milošević in 1999 when we provided shelter for nearly 400,000 refugees. Yet we managed to pass beyond all these troubles and obstacles along the way in a remarkable manner.

But, in 2001, we faced the greatest challenge and threat in our existence as a country. The people and the political leadership of the Republic of Macedonia were again strong enough and united. Apart from preserving the integrity of the country, at the same time we achieved democratic reforms that were unique: we succeeded in transforming the conflict into political dialogue and managed to usher its negative consequences into the institutions of our open system, and that never happened before in former Yugoslavia.

These achievements seem proof of the democratic credentials of our country and the political maturity of the overwhelming majority of our citizens who remained firm in preserving the peace and values of living together. The Framework Agreement is one proof of the strength of our multiethnic democracy and a template for other countries in the larger region for resolving the problems in the area of interethnic relations and in setting up unprecedented high standards of educational, linguistic, and cultural rights for the members of these various ethnic communities.

NOTE

*A copy of this analysis in ".pdf" format is available online at: http://www.iri.org/pdfs/MK_Exit_Poll.pdf

Appendix C

The Constitution of the Republic of Macedonia and Amendments

This document reflects the orginal 134 Articles of the constitution of 8 September 1991, as well as the first two amendments of the Constitution, which were amended on 6 January 1992, partially to allay Greek accusations of Macedonian claims on soverign Greek territory. (Notably, this was one of the few examples in history where an independent state voluntarily modified its constitution to accomodate the concerns of a neighboring state.) Amendment III was added later at an unspecificed date, and Amendments IV through XVIII were added after the signing of the Ohrid Framework Agreement (on 13 August 2001) on 16 November 2001.

Taking as the points of departure the historical, cultural, spiritual and statehood heritage of the Macedonian people and their struggle over centuries for national and social freedom as well as the creation of their own state, and particularly the traditions of statehood and legality of the Kruševo Republic and the historic decisions of the Anti-Fascist Assembly of the People's Liberation of Macedonia, together with the constitutional and legal continuity of the Macedonian state as a sovereign republic within Federal Yugoslavia and freely manifested will of the citizens of the Republic of Macedonia in the referendum of September 8th, 1991, as well as the historical fact that Macedonia is established as a national state of the Macedonian people, in which full equality as citizens and permanent co-existence with the Macedonian people is provided for Albanians, Turks, Vlachs, Romanics and other nationalities living in the Republic of Macedonia, and intent on:

- the establishment of the Republic of Macedonia as a sovereign and independent state, as well as a civil and democratic one;
- the establishment and consolidation of the rule of law as a fundamental system of government;
- the guaranteeing of human rights, citizens' freedoms and ethnic equality;
- the provision of peace and a common home for the Macedonian people with the nationalities living in the Republic of Macedonia; and on
- the provision of social justice, economic wellbeing and prosperity in the life of the individual and the community,

the Assembly of the Republic of Macedonia adopts.

THE CONSTITUTION OF THE REPUBLIC OF MACEDONIA

I. BASIC PROVISIONS

Article 1

The Republic of Macedonia is a sovereign, independent, democratic and social state.

The sovereignty of the Republic of Macedonia is indivisible, inalienable and nontransferable.

Article 2

Sovereignty in the Republic of Macedonia derives from the citizens and belongs to the citizens.

The citizens of the Republic of Macedonia exercise their authority through democratically elected Representatives through referendum and through other forms of direct expression.

Article 3

The territory of the Republic of Macedonia is indivisible and inviolable.

The existing borders of the Republic of Macedonia are inviolable. The borders of the Republic of Macedonia may be changed only in accordance with the constitution.

Article 4

Citizens of the Republic of Macedonia have citizenship of the Republic of Macedonia.

A subject of the Republic of Macedonia may neither be deprived of citizenship, nor expelled or extradited to another state.

Citizenship of the Republic of Macedonia is regulated by law.

Article 5

The state symbols of the Republic of Macedonia are the coat of arms, the flag and the national anthem. The coat of arms, the flag and the national anthem of the Republic of Macedonia are adopted by law by a two-thirds majority vote of the total number of Assembly Representatives.

Article 6

The Capital of the Republic of Macedonia is Skopje.

Article 7

The Macedonian language, written using its Cyrillic alphabet, is the official language in the Republic of Macedonia. In the units of local self-government where the majority of the inhabitants belong to a nationality, in addition to the Macedonian language and Cyrillic alphabet, their language and alphabet are also in official use, in a manner determined by law. In the units of local self-government where there is a considerable number of inhabitants belonging to a nationality, their language and alphabet are also in official use, in addition to the Macedonian language and Cyrillic alphabet, under conditions and in a manner determined by law.

Article 8

The fundamental values of the constitutional order of the Republic of Macedonia are:

- the basic freedoms and rights of the individual and citizen, recognised in international law and set down in the Constitution;
- the free expression of national identity;
- the rule of law;
- the division of state powers into legislative, executive and judicial;
- the legal protection of property;

- the freedom of the market and entrepreneurship;
- humanism, social justice and solidarity;
- local self-government;
- proper urban and rural planning to promote a congenial human environment, as well as ecological protection and development; and
- respect for the generally accepted norms of international law.

Anything that is not prohibited by the Constitution or by law is permitted in the Republic of Macedonia.

II. BASIC FREEDOMS AND RIGHTS OF THE INDIVIDUAL AND CITIZEN

1. Civil and Political Freedoms and Rights

Article 9

Citizens of the Republic of Macedonia are equal in their freedoms and rights, regardless of sex, race, color of skin, national and social origin, political and religious beliefs, property and social status.

All citizens are equal before the Constitution and law.

Article 10

The human right to life is irrevocable.

The death penalty shall not be imposed on any grounds whatsoever in the Republic of Macedonia.

Article 11

The human right to physical and moral dignity is irrevocable.

Any form of torture, or inhuman or humiliating conduct or punishment, is prohibited.

Forced labor is prohibited.

Article 12

The human right to freedom is irrevocable.

No person's freedom can be restricted except by court decision or in cases and procedures determined by law.

Persons summoned, apprehended or detained shall immediately be informed of the reasons for the summons, apprehension or detention and on their rights. They shall not be forced to make a statement. A person has a right to an attorney in police and court procedure.

Persons detained shall be brought before a court as soon as possible, within a maximum period of 24 hours from the moment of detention, and the legality of their detention shall there be decided upon without delay.

Detention may last, by court decision, for a maximum of 90 days from the day of detention.

Persons detained may, under the conditions determined by law, be released from custody to conduct their defence.

Article 13

A person indicted for an offence shall be considered innocent until his/her guilt is established by a legally valid court verdict. A person unlawfully detained, apprehended or convicted has a right to legal redress and other rights determined by law.

Article 14

No person may be punished for an offence which has not been declared an offence punishable by law, or by other acts, prior to its being committed, and for which no punishment has been prescribed. No person may be tried in a court of law for an offence of which he/she has already been tried and for which a legally valid court verdict has already been brought.

Article 15

The right to appeal against individual legal acts issued in a first instance proceedings by a court, administrative body, organisation or other institution carrying out public mandates is guaranteed.

Article 16

The freedom of personal conviction, conscience, thought and public expression of thought is guaranteed.

The freedom of speech, public address, public information and the establishment of institutions for public information is guaranteed.

Free access to information and the freedom of reception and transmission of information are guaranteed.

The right of reply via the mass media is guaranteed.

The right to a correction in the mass media is guaranteed.

The right to protect a source of information in the mass media is guaranteed.

Censorship is prohibited.

Article 17

The freedom and confidentiality of correspondence and other forms of communication is guaranteed.

Only a court decision may authorise nonapplication of the principle of the inviolability of the confidentiality of correspondence and other forms of communication, in cases where it is indispensable to a criminal investigation or required in the interests of the defence of the Republic.

Article 18

The security and confidentiality of personal information are guaranteed.

Citizens are guaranteed protection from any violation of their personal integrity deriving from the registration of personal information through data processing.

Article 19

The freedom of religious confession is guaranteed.

The right to express one's faith freely and publicly, individually or with others is guaranteed.

The Macedonian Orthodox Church and other religious communities and groups are free to establish schools and other social and charitable institutions, by ways of a procedure regulated by law.

Article 20

Citizens are guaranteed freedom of association to exercise and protect their political, economic, social, cultural and other rights and convictions.

Citizens may freely establish associations of citizens and political parties, join them or resign from them.

The programs and activities of political parties and other associations of citizens may not be directed at the violent destruction of the constitutional order of the Republic, or at encouragement or incitement to military aggression or ethnic, racial or religious hatred or intolerance.

Military or paramilitary associations which do not belong to the Armed Forces of the Republic of Macedonia are prohibited.

Article 21

Citizens have the right to assemble peacefully and to express public protest without prior announcement or a special licence. The exercise of this right may be restricted only during a state of emergency or war.

Article 22

Every citizen on reaching 18 years of age acquires the right to vote. The right to vote is equal, universal and direct, and is exercised at free elections by secret ballot.

Persons deprived of the right to practise their profession by a court verdict do not have the right to vote.

Article 23

Every citizen has the right to take part in the performance of public office.

Article 24

Every citizen has a right to petition state and other public bodies, as well as to receive an answer.

A citizen cannot be called to account or suffer adverse consequences for attitudes expressed in petitions, unless they entail the committing of a criminal offence.

Article 25

Each citizen is guaranteed the respect and protection of the privacy of his/her personal and family life and his/her dignity and repute.

Article 26

The inviolability of the home is guaranteed.

The right to the inviolability of the home may be restricted only by a court decision in cases of the detection or prevention of criminal offences or the protection of people's health.

Article 27

Every citizen of the Republic of Macedonia has the right of free movement on the territory of the Republic and freely to choose his/her place of residence.

Every citizen has the right to leave the territory of the Republic and to return to the Republic.

The exercise of these rights may be restricted by law only in cases where it is necessary for the protection of the security of the Republic, criminal investigation or protection of people's health.

Article 28

The defence of the Republic of Macedonia is the right and duty of every citizen.

The exercise of this right and duty of citizens is regulated by law.

Article 29

Foreign subjects enjoy freedoms and rights guaranteed by the Constitution in the Republic of Macedonia, under conditions regulated by law and international agreements.

The Republic guarantees the right of asylum to foreign subjects and stateless persons expelled because of democratic political convictions and activities.

Extradition of a foreign subject can be carried out only on a basis of a ratified international agreement and on the principle of reciprocity. A foreign subject cannot be extradited for political criminal offences. Acts of terrorism are not regarded as political criminal offences.

2. Economic, Social and Cultural Rights

Article 30

The right to ownership of property and the right of inheritance are guaranteed.

Ownership of property creates rights and duties and should serve the wellbeing of both the individual and the community. No person may be deprived of his/her property or of the rights deriving from it, except in cases concerning the public interest determined by law.

If property is expropriated or restricted, rightful compensation not lower than its market value is guaranteed.

Article 31

Foreign subjects in the Republic of Macedonia may acquire the right of ownership of property under conditions determined by law.

Article 32

Everyone has the right to work, to free choice of employment, protection at work and material assistance during temporary unemployment.

Every job is open to all under equal conditions. Every employee has a right to appropriate remuneration. Every employee has the right to paid daily, weekly and annual leave. Employees cannot waive this right.

The exercise of the rights of employees and their positions are regulated by law and collective agreements.

Article 33

Everyone is obliged to pay tax and other public contributions, as well as to share in the discharge of public expenditure in a manner determined by law.

Article 34

Citizens have a right to social security and social insurance, determined by law and collective agreement.

Article 35

The Republic provides for the social protection and social security of citizens in accordance with the principle of social justice.

The Republic guarantees the right of assistance to citizens who are infirm or unfit for work.

The Republic provides particular protection for invalid persons, as well as conditions for their involvement in the life of the society.

Article 36

The Republic guarantees particular social security rights to veterans of the Anti-Fascist War and of all Macedonian national liberation wars, to war invalids, to those expelled and imprisoned for the ideas of the separate identity of the Macedonian people and of Macedonian statehood, as well as to members of their families without means of material and social subsistence.

The particular rights are regulated by law.

Article 37

In order to exercise their economic and social rights, citizens have the right to establish trade unions. Trade unions can constitute confederations and become members of international trade union organisations.

The law may restrict the conditions for the exercise of the right to trade union organisation in the armed forces, the police and administrative bodies.

Article 38

The right to strike is guaranteed.

The law may restrict the conditions for the exercise of the right to strike in the armed forces, the police and administrative bodies.

Article 39

Every citizen is guaranteed the right to health care.

Citizens have the right and duty to protect and promote their own health and the health of others.

Article 40

The Republic provides particular care and protection for the family. The legal relations in marriage, the family and cohabitation are regulated by law.

Parents have the right and duty to provide for the nurturing and education of their children. Children are responsible for the care of their old and infirm parents.

The Republic provides particular protection for parentless children and children without parental care.

Article 41

It is a human right freely to decide on the procreation of children.

The Republic conducts a humane population policy in order to provide balanced economic and social development.

Article 42

The Republic particularly protects mothers, children and minors. A person under 15 years of age cannot be employed.

Minors and mothers have the right to particular protection at work. Minors may not be employed in work which is detrimental to their health or morality.

Article 43

Everyone has the right to a healthy environment to live in.

Everyone is obliged to promote and protect the environment.

The Republic provides conditions for the exercise of the right of citizens to a healthy environment.

Article 44

Everyone has a right to education.

Education is accessible to everyone under equal conditions.

Primary education is compulsory and free.

Article 45

Citizens have a right to establish private schools at all levels of education, with the exception of primary education, under conditions determined by law.

Article 46

The autonomy of universities is guaranteed.

The conditions of establishment, performance and termination of the activities of a university are regulated by law.

Article 47

The freedom of scholarly, artistic and other forms of creative work is guaranteed.

Rights deriving from scholarly, artistic or other intellectual creative work are guaranteed.

The Republic stimulates, assists and protects the development of scholarship, the arts and culture.

The Republic stimulates and assists scientific and technological development.

The Republic stimulates and assists technical education and sport.

Article 48

Members of nationalities have a right freely to express, foster and develop their identity and national attributes.

The Republic guarantees the protection of the ethnic, cultural, linguistic and religious identity of the nationalities.

Members of the nationalities have the right to establish institutions for culture and art, as well as scholarly and other associations for the expression, fostering and development of their identity.

Members of the nationalities have the right to instruction in their language in primary and secondary education, as determined by law. In schools where education is carried out in the language of a nationality, the Macedonian language is also studied.

Article 49

The Republic cares for the status and rights of those persons belonging to the Macedonian people in neighboring countries, as well as Macedonian expatriates, assists their cultural development and promotes links with them.

The Republic cares for the cultural, economic and social rights of the citizens of the Republic abroad.

3. Guarantees of Basic Freedoms and Rights

Article 50

Every citizen may invoke the protection of freedoms and rights determined by the Constitution before the regular courts, as well as before the Constitutional Court of Macedonia, through a procedure based upon the principles of priority and urgency.

Judicial protection of the legality of individual acts of state administration, as well as of other institutions carrying out public mandates, is guaranteed.

A citizen has the right to be informed on human rights and basic freedoms as well as actively to contribute, individually or jointly with others, to their promotion and protection.

Article 51

In the Republic of Macedonia laws shall be in accordance with the Constitution and all other regulations in accordance with the Constitution and law.

Everyone is obliged to respect the Constitution and the laws.

Article 52

Laws and other regulations are published before they come into force. Laws and other regulations are published in 'The Official Gazette of the Republic of Macedonia' at most seven days after the day of their adoption.

Laws come into force on the eighth day after the day of their republication at the earliest, or on the day of publication in exceptional cases determined by the Assembly.

Laws and other regulations may not have a retroactive effect, except in cases when this is more favorable for the citizens.

Article 53

Attorneyship is an autonomous and independent public service, providing a legal assistance and carrying out public mandates in accordance with the law.

Article 54

The freedoms and rights of the individual and citizen can be restricted only in cases determined by the Constitution. The freedoms and rights of the individual and citizen can be restricted during states of war or emergency, in accordance with the provisions of the Constitution.

The restriction of freedoms and rights cannot discriminate on grounds of sex, race, color of skin, language, religion, national or social origin, property or social status.

The restriction of freedoms and rights cannot be applied to the right to life, the interdiction of torture, inhuman and humiliating conduct and punishment, the legal determination of punishable offences and sentences, as well as to the freedom of personal conviction, conscience, thought and religious confession.

4. Foundations for Economic Relations

Article 55

The freedom of the market and entrepreneurship is guaranteed.

The Republic ensures an equal legal position to all parties in the market. The Republic takes measures against monopolistic positions and monopolistic conduct on the market.

The freedom of the market and entrepreneurship can be restricted by law only for reasons of the defence of the Republic, protection of the natural and living environment or public health.

Article 56

All the natural resources of the Republic of Macedonia, the flora and fauna, amenities in common use, as well as the objects and buildings of particular cultural and historical value determined by law, are amenities of common interest for the Republic and enjoy particular protection.

The Republic guarantees the protection, promotion and enhancement of the historical and artistic heritage of the Macedonian people and of the nationalities and the treasures of which it is composed, regardless of their legal status. The law regulates the mode and conditions under which specific items of general interest for the Republic can be ceded for use.

Article 57

The Republic of Macedonia stimulates economic progress and provides for a more balanced spatial and regional development, as well as for the more rapid development of economically underdeveloped regions.

Article 58

Ownership and labor form the basis for management and sharing in decisionmaking.

Participation in management and decisionmaking in public institutions and services is regulated by law, on the principles of expertise and competence.

Article 59

Foreign investors are guaranteed the right to the free transfer of invested capital and profits.

The rights obtained on the basis of the capital invested may not be reduced by law or other regulations.

Article 60

The National Bank of the Republic of Macedonia is a currency-issuing bank.

The National Bank is autonomous and responsible for the stability of the currency, monetary policy and for the general liquidity of payments in the Republic and abroad.

The organisation and work of the National Bank are regulated by law.

III. THE ORGANISATION OF STATE AUTHORITY

1. The Assembly of the Republic of Macedonia

Article 61

The Assembly of the Republic of Macedonia is a representative body of the citizens and the legislative power of the Republic is vested in it. The organisation and functioning of the Assembly are regulated by the Constitution and by the Rules of Procedure.

Article 62

The Assembly of the Republic of Macedonia is composed of 120 to 140 Representatives.

The Representatives are elected at general, direct and free elections and by secret ballot.

The Representatives represents the citizens and makes decisions in the Assembly in accordance with his/her personal convictions.

A Representative's mandate cannot be revoked.

The mode and conditions of election of Representatives are regulated by a law adopted by a two-thirds majority vote of the total number of Representatives.

Article 63

The Representatives for the Assembly are elected for a term of four years. The mandate of Representatives is verified by the Assembly. The length of the mandate is reckoned from the constitutive meeting of the Assembly. Each newly elected Assembly must hold a constitutive meeting 20 days at the latest after the election was held. The constitutive meeting is called by the President of the Assembly of the previous term.

If a constitutive meeting is not called within the time laid down, the Representatives assemble and constitute the Assembly themselves on the twenty-first day after the completion of the elections. Elections for Representatives to the Assembly are held within the last 90 days of the term of the current Assembly, or within 60 days from the day the dissolution of the Assembly.

The term of office of the Representatives to the Assembly can be extended only during states of war or emergency.

Cases where a citizen cannot be elected a Representative, owing to the incompatibility of this office with other public offices or professions already held, are defined by law. The Assembly is dissolved when more than half of the total number of Representatives vote for dissolution.

Article 64

Representatives enjoy immunity.

A Representative cannot be held to have committed a criminal offence or be detained owing to views he/she has expressed or to the way he/she has voted in the Assembly.

A Representative cannot be detained without the approval of the Assembly unless found committing a criminal offence for which a prison sentence of at least five years is prescribed. The Assembly can decide to invoke immunity for a Representative without his/her request, should it be necessary for the performance of the Representative's office.

Representatives may not be called up for duties in the Armed Forces during the course of their term of office.

A Representative is entitled to remuneration determined by law.

Article 65

A Representative may resign his/her mandate.

The Representative submits his/her resignation in person at a session of the Assembly.

The mandate of a Representative terminates if he/she is sentenced for a criminal offence for which a prison sentence of at least five years is prescribed.

The Representative can have his/her mandate revoked for committing a criminal offence making him/her unfit to perform the office of a Representative, as well as for absence from the Assembly for longer than 6 months for no justifiable reason. Revocation of the mandate is determined by the Assembly by a two-thirds majority vote of all Representatives.

Article 66

The Assembly is in permanent session.

The Assembly works at meetings.

The meetings of the Assembly are called by the President of the Assembly.

The Assembly adopts the Rules of Procedure by a two-thirds majority vote of the total number of Representatives.

Article 67

The Assembly elects a President and one or more Vice-Presidents from the ranks of the Representatives by a majority vote of the total number of Representatives.

The President of the Assembly represents the Assembly, ensures the application of the Rules of Procedure and carries out other responsibilities determined by the Constitution and the Rules of Procedure of the Assembly.

The office of the President of the Assembly is incompatible with the performance of other public offices, professions or appointment in a political party.

The President of the Assembly issues notice to the election of Representatives and of the President of the Republic.

Article 68

The Assembly of the Republic of Macedonia

- adopts and changes the Constitution;
- adopts laws and gives the authentic interpretation of laws;
- determines public taxes and fees;

- adopts the budget and the balance of payments of the Republic;
- adopts the spatial plan of the Republic;
- ratifies international agreements;
- decides on war and peace;
- makes decisions concerning any changes in the borders of the Republic;
- makes decisions on association in the disassociation from any form of union or community with other states;
- issues notice of a referendum;
- makes decisions concerning the reserves of the Republic;
- sets up councils;
- elects the Government of the Republic of Macedonia;
- carries out elections and discharges judges;
- selects, appoints and dismisses other holders of public and other offices determined by the Constitution and law;
- carries out political monitoring and supervision of the Government and other holders of public office responsible to the Assembly;
- proclaims amnesties; and
- performs other activities determined by the Constitution.

In carrying out the duties within its sphere of competence, the Assembly adopts decisions, declarations, resolutions, recommendations and conclusions.

Article 69

The Assembly may work if its meeting is attended by a majority of the total number of Representatives. The Assembly makes decisions by a majority vote of the Representatives attending, but no less than one-third of the total number of Representatives, in so far as the Constitution does not provide for a qualified majority.

Article 70

The meetings of the Assembly are open to the public.

The Assembly may decide to work without the presence of the public by a two-thirds majority vote of the total number of Representatives.

Article 71

The right to propose adoption of a law is given to every Representative of the Assembly, to the Government of the Republic and to a group of at least 10,000 voters.

The initiative for adopting a law may be given to the authorised instances by any citizen, group of citizens, institutions or associations.

Article 72

An interpellation may be made concerning the work of any public office-holder, the Government and any of its members individually, as well as on issues concerning the performance of state bodies.

Interpellations may be made by a minimum of five Representatives.

All Representatives have the right to ask a Representative's question. The mode and procedure for submitting and debating on an interpellation and Representative's question are regulated by the Rules of Procedure.

Article 73

The Assembly decides on issuing notice of a referendum concerning specific matters within its sphere of competence by a majority vote of the total number of Representatives.

The decision of the majority of votes in a referendum is adopted on condition that more than half of the total number of voters voted. The Assembly is obliged to issue notice of a referendum if one is proposed by at least 150,000 voters.

The decision made in a referendum is binding.

Article 74

The Assembly makes decisions on any change in the borders of the Republic of Macedonia by a two-thirds majority vote of the total number of Representatives.

The decision on any change in the borders of the Republic is adopted by referendum, in so far as it is accepted by the majority of the total number of voters.

Article 75

Laws are declared by promulgation.

The promulgation declaring a law is signed by the President of the Republic and the President of the Assembly.

The President of the Republic may decide not to sign the promulgation declaring a law. The Assembly considers the President of the Republic is then obligated to sign the promulgation in so far as it is adopted by a majority vote of the total number of Representatives.

The President is obligated to sign a promulgation if the law has been adopted by a two-thirds majority vote of the total number of Representatives in accordance with the Constitution.

Article 76

The Assembly sets up permanent and temporary working bodies. The Assembly may set up survey commissions for any domain or any matter of public interest.

A proposal for setting up a survey of commission may be submitted by a minimum of 20 Representatives.

The Assembly sets up a permanent survey commission for the protection of the freedoms and rights of citizens.

The findings of the survey commissions form the basis for the initiation of proceedings to ascertain the answerability of public office-holders.

Article 77

The Assembly elects the Public Attorney.

The Public Attorney protects the constitutional and legal rights of citizens when violated by bodies of state administration and by other bodies and organisations with public mandates.

The Public Attorney is elected for a term of eight years, with the right to one reelection.

The conditions for election and dismissal, the sphere of competence and the mode of work of the Public Attorney are regulated by law.

Article 78

The Assembly establishes a Council for Inter-Ethnic Relations. The Council consists of the President of the Assembly and two members each from the ranks of the Macedonians, Albanians, Turks, Vlachs and Romanies, as well as two members from the ranks of other nationalities in Macedonia.

The President of the Assembly is President of the Council. The Assembly elects the members of the Council.

The Council considers issues of inter-ethnic relations in the Republic and makes appraisals and proposals for their solution.

The Assembly is obliged to take into consideration the appraisals and proposals of the Council and to make decisions regarding them.

2. The President of the Republic of Macedonia

Article 79

The President of the Republic of Macedonia represents the Republic. The President of the Republic is Commander-in-Chief of the Armed Forces of Macedonia.

The President of the Republic exercises his/her rights and duties on the basis and within the framework of the Constitution and laws.

Article 80

The President of the Republic of elected is general and directs elections, by secret ballot, for a term of five years. A person may be elected President of the Republic of Macedonia two times at most.

The President of the Republic shall be a citizen of the Republic of Macedonia.

A person may be elected President of the Republic if over the age of 40 on the day of election.

A person may not be elected President of the Republic if, on the day of the election, he/she has not been a resident of the Republic of Macedonia for at least ten years within the last fifteen years.

Article 81

A candidate for President of the Republic can be nominated by a minimum of 10,000 voters or at least 30 Representatives. A candidate for President of the Republic is elected if voted by a majority of the total number of voters.

If in the first round of voting no candidate wins the majority required, voting in the second round is restricted to the two candidates who have won most votes in the first round.

The second round takes place within 14 days of the termination of voting in the first round.

A candidate is elected President if he/she wins a majority of the votes of those who voted, provided more than half of the registered voters voted.

If in the second round of voting no candidate wins the required majority of votes, the whole electoral procedure is repeated.

If only one candidate is nominated for the post of President of the Republic and he/she does not obtain the required majority of votes in the first round, the whole electoral procedure is repeated.

The election of the President of the Republic takes place within the last 60 days of the term of the previous President. Should the term of office of the President of the Republic be terminated for any reason, the election of a new President takes place within 40 days from the day of termination.

Before taking up office, the President of the Republic of Macedonia makes a solemn declaration before the Assembly of his/her commitment to respect the Constitution and laws.

Article 82

In case of death, resignation, permanent inability to perform his/her duties, or in case of termination of the mandate in accordance with the provisions of the Constitution, the office of the President of the Republic is carried out by the President of the Assembly until the election of the new President.

Decisions on the applicability of the conditions for the occasion of the office of the President of the Republic are the official duty of the Constitutional Court.

Should the President of the Republic be temporarily unable to preform his/her duties, the President of the Assembly deputises for him/her. While the President of the Assembly is performing the office of President of the Republic, he/she takes part in the work of the Assembly without the right to vote.

Article 83

The duty of the President of the Republic is incompatible with the performance of any other public office, profession or appointment in a political party.

The President of the Republic is granted immunity.

The Constitutional Court decides by a two-thirds majority vote of the total number and approving of detention for the President of the Republic.

Article 84

The President of the Republic of Macedonia

- nominates a mandator to constitute the Government of the Republic of Macedonia;
- appoints and dismisses by decree ambassadors and other diplomatic representatives of the Republic of Macedonia abroad;
- accepts the credentials and letters of recall of foreign diplomatic representatives;
- proposes two judges to sit on the Constitutional Court of the Republic of Macedonia;

- proposes two members of the Republican Judicial Council;
- appoints three members to the Security Council of the Republic of Macedonia;
- proposes the members of the Council for Inter-Ethnic Relations;
- appoints and dismisses other holders of state and public office determined by the Constitution and the law;
- grants decorations and honours in accordance with the law;
- grants pardons in accordance with the law; and
- performs other duties determined by the Constitution.

Article 85

The President of the Republic addresses the Assembly on issues within his/her sphere of competence at least once a year.

The Assembly may request the President of the Republic to state an opinion on issues within his/her sphere of competence.

Article 86

The President of the republic is President of the Security Council of the Republic of Macedonia.

The Security Council of the Republic is composed of the President of the Republic, the President of the Assembly, the Prime Minister, the Ministers heading the bodies of state administration in the fields of security, defence and foreign affairs and three members appointed by the President of the Republic.

The Council considers issues relating to the security and defence of the Republic and makes policy proposals to the Assembly and the Government.

Article 87

The President is held accountable for any violations of the Constitution in exercising his/her rights and duties.

The procedure for determining the President of the Republic's answerability is initiated by the Assembly with a two-thirds majority vote of all Representatives.

It is the Constitutional Court that decides on the answerability of the President by a two-thirds majority vote of all judges.

If the Constitutional Court considers the President answerable for a violation, his/her mandate is terminated by the force of the Constitution.

3. The Government of the Republic of Macedonia

Article 88

Executive power is vested in the Government of the Republic of Macedonia.

The Government exercises its rights and competence on the basis and within the framework of the Constitution and law.

Article 89

The Government is composed of a Prime Minister and Ministers. The Prime Minister and the Ministers cannot be Representatives in the Assembly.

The Prime Minister, Deputy Prime Ministers and Ministers are guaranteed immunity. The Government decides on their immunity. The Prime Minister, Deputy Prime Ministers and Ministers cannot be called up for duties in the Armed Forces.

The office of Prime Minister or Minister is incompatible with any other public office or profession.

The organisation and mode of working of the Government are regulated by law.

Article 90

The President of the Republic of Macedonia is obliged, within 10 days of the constitution of the Assembly, to entrust the mandate for constituting the Government to a candidate from the party or parties which has/have a majority in the Assembly.

Within 20 days from the day of being entrusted with the mandate, the mandator submits a program to the Assembly and proposes the composition of the Government.

The Government is elected by the Assembly on the proposal of the mandator and on the basis of the program by a majority vote of the total number of Representatives.

Article 91

The Government of the Republic of Macedonia

- determines the policy of carrying out the laws and other regulations of the Assembly and is responsible for their execution;
- proposes laws, the budget of the Republic and other regulations adopted by the Assembly;

- proposes a spatial plan of the Republic;
- proposes decisions concerning the reserves of the Republic and sees to their execution;
- adopts by laws and other acts for the execution of laws;
- lays down principles on the internal organisation and work of the Ministries and other administrative bodies, directing and supervising their work;
- provides appraisals of drafts of laws and other acts submitted to the Assembly by other authorised bodies;
- decides on the recognition of states and governments;
- establishes diplomatic and consular relations with other states;
- makes a decision on opening diplomatic and consular offices abroad;
- proposes the appointment of ambassadors and Representatives of the Republic of Macedonia abroad and appoints chiefs of consular offices;
- proposes the Public Prosecutor;
- appoints and dismisses holders of public and other office determined by the Constitution and laws; and
- performs other duties determined by the Constitution and law.

Article 92

The Government and each of its members are accountable to the Assembly.

The Assembly may take a vote of no-confidence in the Government. A vote of no-confidence in the Government may be initiated by a minimum of 20 Representatives.

The vote of no-confidence in the Government is taken after three days have elapsed since the last vote, unless proposed by a majority of all Representatives.

A vote of no-confidence in the Government is adopted by a majority vote of all the Representatives. If a vote of no-confidence in the Government is passed, the Government is obliged to submit its resignation.

Article 93

The Government itself has the right to raise the question of confidence before the Assembly.

The Government has the right to submit its resignation. The resignation of the Prime Minister, his/her death or permanent inability to perform his/her duties entail the resignation of the Government.

The Government ceases its term of office when the Assembly is dissolved.

When a vote of no-confidence in the Government has been passed, it has submitted its resignation, or its term of office has ceased owing to the dissolution of the Assembly, the same Government remains on duty until the election of a new Government.

Article 94

A member of the Government has the right to submit his/her resignation.

The Prime Minister may propose the dismissal of a member of the Government.

The Assembly decides on the proposal for the dismissal of a member of the Government at its first meeting following the proposal. If the Prime Minister dismisses more than one-third of the initial composition of the Government, the Assembly follows the same procedure as for the election of a new Government.

Article 95

The state administration consists of Ministers and other administrative bodies and organisations determined by law. Political organisation and activities within bodies of state administration are regulated by a law to be adopted by a two-thirds majority vote of all Representatives.

Article 96

The bodies of state administration perform the duties within their sphere of competence autonomously and on the basis and within the framework of the Constitution and laws, being accountable for their work to the Government.

Article 97

The bodies of state administration in the fields of defence and the police are to be headed by civilians who have been civilians for at least three years before their election to these offices.

4. The Judiciary

Article 98

Judiciary power is exercised by courts.

Courts are autonomous and independent. Courts judge on the basis of the Constitution and laws and international agreements ratified in accordance with the Constitution.

There is one form of organisation for the judiciary.

Emergency courts are prohibited.

The types of courts, their spheres of competence, their establishment, abrogation, organisation and composition, as well as the procedure they follow are regulated by a law adopted by a majority vote of two-thirds of the total number of Representatives.

Article 99

A judge is elected without restriction of his/her term of office.

A judge cannot be transferred against his/her will.

A judge is discharged

- if he/she so requests;
- if he/she permanently loses the capability of carrying out a judge's office, which is determined by the Republican Judicial Council;
- if he/she fulfils the conditions for retirement;
- if he/she is sentenced for a criminal offence to a prison term of a minimum of six months;
- owing to a serious disciplinary offence defined in law, making him/her unsuitable to perform a judge's office as decided by the Republican Judicial Council; and
- owing to unprofessional and unethical performance of a judge's office, as decided by the Republican Judicial Council in a procedure regulated by law.

Article 100

Judges are granted immunity.

The Assembly decides on the immunity of judges.

The performance of a judge's office is incompatible with other public office, profession or membership in a political party.

Political organisation and activity in the judiciary is prohibited.

Article 101

The Supreme Court of Macedonia is the highest court in the Republic, providing uniformity in the implementation of the laws by the courts.

Article 102

Court hearings and the passing of verdicts are public.

The public can be excluded in cases determined by law.

Article 103

The court tries cases in council.

The law determined cases in which a judge can sit alone.

Jury judges take part in a trial in cases determined by law.

Jury judges cannot be held answerable for their opinions and decisions concerning their verdict.

Article 104

The Republican Judicial Council is composed of seven members.

The Assembly elects the members of the Council.

The members of the Council are elected from the ranks of outstanding members of the legal profession for a term of six years with the right to one reelection.

Members of the Republican Judicial Council are granted immunity. The Assembly decides on their immunity.

The office of a member of the Republican Judicial Council is incompatible with the performance of other public offices, professions or membership in political parties.

Article 105

The Republican Judicial Council

- proposes to the Assembly the election and discharge of judges and determines proposals for the discharge of a judge's office in cases laid down in the Constitution;
- decides on the disciplinary answerability of judges;
- assesses the competence and ethics of judges in the performance of their office; and
- proposes two judges to sit on the Constitutional Court of Macedonia.

5. The Public Prosecutor's Office

Article 106

The Public Prosecutor's Office is a single and autonomous state body carrying out legal measures against persons who have committed criminal and other offences determined by law; it also performs other duties determined by law.

The Public Prosecutor's Office carries out its duties on the basis of and within the framework of the Constitution and law. The Public Prosecutor is appointed by the Assembly for a term of six years and is discharged by the Assembly.

Article 107

The Public Prosecutor is granted immunity.

The Assembly decides on his/her immunity.

The office of the Public Prosecutor is incompatible with the performance of any other public office, profession or membership in a political party.

IV. THE CONSTITUTIONAL COURT OF MACEDONIA

Article 108

The Constitutional Court of Macedonia is a body of the Republic protecting constitutionality and legality.

Article 109

The Constitutional Court of Macedonia is composed of nine judges. The Assembly elects the judges to the Constitutional Court by a majority vote of the total number of Representatives. The term of office of the judges is nine years without the right to reelection. The Constitutional Court elects a President from its own ranks for a term of three years without the right to reelection.

Judges of the Constitutional Court are elected from the ranks of outstanding members of the legal profession.

Article 110

The Constitutional Court of Macedonia

- decides on the conformity of laws with the Constitution;
- decides on the conformity of collective agreements and other regulations with the Constitution and laws;
- protects the freedoms and rights of the individual and citizen relating to the freedom of communication, conscience, thought and activity as well as to the prohibition of discrimination among citizens on the grounds of sex, race, religion or national, social or political affiliation;
- decides on conflicts of competency among holders of legislative, executive and judicial offices;
- decides on conflicts of competency among Republic bodies and units of local self-government;
- decides on the answerability of the programs and status of political parties and associations of citizens; and
- decides on other issues determined by the Constitution.

Article 111

The office of judge of the Constitutional Court is incompatible with the performance of other public office, profession or membership in a political party.

Judges of the Constitutional Court are granted immunity. The Constitutional Court decides on their immunity. Judges of the Constitutional Court cannot be called up for duties in the Armed Forces.

The office of a judge of the Constitutional Court ceases when the incumbent resigns. A judge of the Constitutional Court shall be discharged from office if sentenced for a criminal offence to unconditional imprisonment of a minimum of six months, or if he/she permanently loses the capability of performing his/her office, as determined by the Constitutional Court.

Article 112

The Constitutional Court shall repeal or invalidate a law if it determines that the law does not conform to the Constitution. The Constitutional Court shall repeal or invalidate a collective agreement, other regulation or enactment, statue or programme of a political party or association, if it determines that the same does not conform to the Constitution or law. The decisions of the Constitutional Court are final and executive.

Article 113

The mode of work and the procedure of the Constitutional Court are regulated by the enactment of the Court.

V. LOCAL SELF-GOVERNMENT

Article 114

The right of citizens to local self-government is guaranteed. Municipalities are units of local self-government.

Within municipalities forms of neighbourhood self-government may be established.

Municipalities are financed from their own sources of income determined by law as well as by funds from the Republic.

Local self-government is regulated by a law adopted by a two-thirds majority of the total number of Representatives.

Article 115

In units of local self-government, citizens directly and through representatives participate in decision making on issues of local relevance particularly in the fields of urban planning, communal activities, culture, sport, social security and child care, preschool education, primary education, basic health care and other fields determined by law.

The municipality is autonomous in the execution of its constitutionally and legally determined spheres of competence; supervision of the legality of its work is carried out by the Republic.

The carrying out of specified matters can by law be entrusted to the municipality by the Republic.

Article 116

The territorial division of the Republic and the area administered by each municipality are defined by law.

Article 117

The City of Skopje is a particular unit of local self-government the organisation of which is regulated by law. In the City of Skopje, citizens directly and through representatives participate in decision making on issues of relevance for the City of Skopje particularly in the field of urban planning, communal activities, culture, sport, social security and child care, preschool education, primary education, basic health care and other fields determined by law.

The City of Skopje is financed from its own sources of income determined by law, as well as by funds from the Republic. The City is autonomous in the execution of its constitutionally and legally determined spheres of competence; supervision of the legality of its work is carried out by the Republic.

By law, the Republic can entrust the carrying out of specified matters to the City.

VI. INTERNATIONAL RELATIONS

Article 118

The international agreements ratified in accordance with the Constitution are part of the internal legal order and cannot be changed by law.

Article 119

International agreement are concludes in the name of the Republic of Macedonia by the President of the Republic of Macedonia. International agreements may also be concludes by the Government of the Republic of Macedonia, when it is so determined by law.

Article 120

A proposal for association in a union or community with other states or for dissociation from a union or community with other states may be submitted by the President of the Republic, the Government or by at least 40 Representatives.

The proposal for association in or dissociation from a union or community with other states is accepted by the Assembly by a two-thirds majority vote of the total number of Representatives. The decision of association in or dissociation from a union or community with other states is adopted if it is upheld in a referendum by the majority of the total number of voters in the Republic.

Article 121

A decision of association or dissociation concerning membership in international organisations is adopted by the Assembly by a majority vote of the total number of Representatives of the Republic, the Government or at least 40 Representatives of the Assembly.

VII. THE DEFENCE OF THE REPUBLIC AND STATES OF WAR AND EMERGENCY

Article 122

The Armed Forces of the Republic of Macedonia protect the territorial integrity and independence of the Republic.

The defence of the Republic is regulated by a law adopted by a two-thirds majority vote to the total number of Representatives.

Article 123

No person is authorised to recognise occupation of the Republic of Macedonia or of part thereof.

Article 124

A state of war exists when direct danger of military attack on the Republic is impending, or when the Republic is attacked, or war is declared on it.

A state of war is declared by the Assembly by a two-thirds majority vote of the total number of Representatives of the Assembly, on the proposal of the President of the Republic, the Government or at least 30 Representatives.

If the Assembly cannot meet, the decision on the declaration of a state of war is made by the President of the Republic who submits it to the Assembly for confirmation as soon as it can meet.

Article 125

A state of emergency exists when major natural disasters or epidemics take place.

A state of emergency on the territory of the Republic of Macedonia or on part thereof is determined by the Assembly on a proposal by the President of the Republic, the Government or by at least 30 Representatives.

The decision to establish the existence of a state of emergency is made by a two-thirds majority vote of the total number of Representatives and can remain in force for a maximum of 30 days. If the Assembly cannot meet, the decision to establish the existence of a state of emergency is made by the President of the Republic, who submits it to the Assembly for confirmation as soon as it can meet.

Article 126

During a state of war or emergency, the Government, in accordance with the Constitution and law, issues decrees with the force of law. The authorisation of the Government to issue decrees with the force of law lasts until the termination of the state of war or emergency, on which the Assembly decides.

Article 127

During a state of war, if the Assembly cannot meet, the President of the Republic may appoint and discharge the Government, as well as appoint or dismiss officials whose election is within the sphere of competence of the Assembly.

Article 128

The mandate of the judges of the Constitutional Court of Macedonia, as well as members of the Republican Judicial Council is extended for the duration of the state of war or emergency.

VIII. CHANGES IN THE CONSTITUTION

Article 129

The Constitution of the Republic of Macedonia can be changed or supplemented by constitutional amendments.

Article 130

A proposal to initiate a change in the Constitution of the Republic of Macedonia may be made by the President of the Republic, by the Government, by at least 30 Representatives, or by 150,000 citizens.

Article 131

The decisions to initiate a change in the Constitution is made by the Assembly by a two-thirds majority vote of the total number of Representatives.

The draft amendment of the Constitution is confirmed by the Assembly by a majority vote of the total number of Representatives and then submitted to public debate.

The decision to change the Constitution is made by the Assembly by a two-thirds majority vote of the total number of Representatives.

The change in the Constitution is declared by the Assembly.

IX. TRANSITIONAL AND FINAL CLAUSES

Article 132

Time of residence in other republics in the Socialist Federal Republic of Yugoslavia is also included in the time span specified in Article 80, Paragraph 5.

Article 133

A Constitution Act shall be adopted for the implementation of the Constitution.

The Constitution Act is adopted by a two-thirds majority vote of the total number of Representatives.

The Constitution Act is declared by the Assembly and comes into force simultaneously with the declaration of the Constitution.

Article 134

This Constitution comes into force on the day it is declared in the Assembly of the Republic of Macedonia.

AMENDMENTS TO THE CONSTITUTION OF THE REPUBLIC OF MACEDONIA

Amendment I

1. The Republic of Macedonia has no territorial pretensions towards any neighbouring state.
2. The borders of the Republic of Macedonia can only be changed in accordance with the Constitution and on the principle of free will, as well in accordance with generally accepted international norms.
3. Clause 1 of this Amendment is an Addendum to Article 3 of the Constitution of the Republic of Macedonia. Clause 2 replaces Paragraph 3 of the same Article.

Amendment II

1. In the exercise of this concern the Republic will not interfere in the sovereign rights of other states or in their internal affairs.
2. This Amendment is an Addendum to Paragraph 1 of Article 49 of the Constitution of the Republic of Macedonia.

These Amendments are an integral part of the Constitution of the Republic of Macedonia and came into force on the day they were promulgated, on January 6th, 1992.

Amendment III

This amendment is part of the Constitution of Republic of Macedonia and it is acting starting with the day of its proclamation.

1. Until the indictment, pretrial detention can last, by court decision, a maximum of 180 days. After the indictment, detention pending trial can be prolonged in a manner and in procedure provided by law.
2. This amendment is replacing paragraph 5 of article 12 of the Constitution of Republic of Macedonia.

Amendment IV

This amendment is part of the Constitution of Republic of Macedonia and it is acting starting with the day of its proclamation on 16th November 2001.

1. The citizens of the Republic of Macedonia, the Macedonian people, as well as the citizens who live inside the border who are a part of the Albanian people, Turkish people, Vlach people, Serbian people, Roma people, Bosnian people and others, taking over the responsibility for the present and the future of their homeland, conscious and thankful to their ancestors for the sacrifice and devotion in their pledge and fight for establishing an independent and sovereign state Macedonia and responsible in front of future generations for retaining and development of everything valuable from the rich cultural inheritance and coexistence in Macedonia, equal in their rights and obligations for common good—republic of Macedonia—in agreement with the tradition of the Krusevo Republic and decisions of ASNOM and of the Referendum dating 8th of September, decided to constitute Republic of Macedonia as independent, sovereign state, with intention to establish and to consolidate the rule of law, to guarantee human rights and citizen's freedom, to establish peace and coexistence, social justice, economic welfare, and progress of the personal and community life, through [its] representatives in the Assembly of Republic of Macedonia, elected on free and democratic elections, issue this[.]

2. With paragraph 1 of this amendment the Preamble of the Constitution of Republic of Macedonia is replaced.

Amendment V

This amendment is part of the Constitution of Republic of Macedonia and it is acting starting with the day of its proclamation on 16th November 2001.

1. The Macedonian language and the Cyrillic letter is the official language throughout the whole territory of Republic of Macedonia and its international relations. Other language spoken by at least 20% of the citizens is also an official language and its letter, as it is determined with this article. Personal IDs, of the citizens that speak a different official language rather than the Macedonian language, are issued in Macedonian language and its letter, as well as in the language that they speak and its letter according to the law. Any citizen that lives in the units of local self-governing in which at least 20% of the citizens speak a different official language rather than the Macedonian language, in communication with regional units of the ministries, can use any of the official languages and its letter. Regional units in charge of those units of the local self-government respond in Macedonian language and its Cyrillic letter, as well as in the official language and letter that is used by the citizen. Any citizen in communication with ministries can use one of the official languages and its letter, and the ministries, will respond in the Macedonian language and its Cyrillic letter, as well as in the official language and letter that is used by the citizen. In

the bodies of the Government of the Republic of Macedonia, the official language different from the Macedonian language can be used according to the law. In the units of the local self-government the language and the letter that is used by at least 20% of the citizens is an official language, beside the Macedonian language and its Cyrillic letter. The decision for use of the languages and letters which are spoken by at least 20% of the citizens in the self-governing units, is made by the bodies of the local self-government units.

2. Article 7 of the Constitution of the Republic of Macedonia is replaced with this amendment.

Amendment VI

This amendment is part of the Constitution of the Republic of Macedonia and it is acting starting with the day of its proclamation on 16th November 2001.

1. Appropriate and fair representation of the citizens that belong in all communities in the bodies of the state government and other public institutions of all levels.
2. Paragraph 2 of article 8 of the Constitution of the Republic of Macedonia is supplemented by this amendment.

Amendment VII

This amendment is part of the Constitution of Republic of Macedonia and it is acting starting with the day of its proclamation on 16th November 2001.

1. The Macedonian Orthodox Church as well as the Islamic Religious Community, Catholic Church, Evangelistic-Methodist Church and Jewish Community, and other religious communities and groups are separated from the state and are equal in front of the law.
2. The Macedonian Orthodox Church as well as the Islamic Religious Community, Catholic Church, Evangelistic-Methodist Church and Jewish Community, and other religious communities and groups are free in establishing of religious schools and social and welfare institutions with procedure regulated by the law.
3. With paragraph 1 of this amendment paragraph 3 of article 19 is replaced, and with paragraph 2 of this amendment paragraph 4 of article 19 of the Constitution of Republic of Macedonia is replaced.

Amendment VIII

This amendment is part of the Constitution of the Republic of Macedonia and it is acting starting with the day of its proclamation 16th November 2001.

1. The members of the communities have the right to freely express, nourish and develop their identity and characteristics of their communities and to use the symbols of their communities. The Republic guaranties protection of the ethnical, cultural, language, and religious identity of all communities. The members of communities have the right to establish cultural, art, educational institutions as well as scientific and other associations for expressing, nourishing and development of their identity. The members of the communities have the right of education in primary and secondary school in their own language according to the law. In schools where the education is taught in another language, the Macedonian language is taught also.

2. Article 48 of the Constitution of Republic of Macedonia is replaced with this amendment.

Amendment IX

This amendment is part of the Constitution of the Republic of Macedonia and it is acting starting with the day of its proclamation 16th November 2001.

1. The Republic guaranties protection, promotion and enrichment of the historical and artistic wealth of Macedonia and of all communities in Macedonia, as well as the treasures which compile it regardless to their legal regime.

2. With this amendment paragraph 2 of article 56 of the Constitution of Republic of Macedonia is replaced.

Amendment X

This amendment is part of the Constitution of the Republic of Macedonia and it is acting starting with the day of its proclamation 16th November 2001.

1. The Assembly can make decisions if the majority of the total number of the representatives are present. The Assembly decides with majority of votes of the present representatives, and with at least one third of the total number of representatives, if a special majority is not predicted by the Constitution.

2. For laws directly concerning culture, use of languages, education, personal IDs and the use of symbols, the Assembly decides from the majority of votes of the present representatives, during which it must have the majority of votes from the present representatives who belong to the communities which are not a majority in the Republic of Macedonia. Controversy in relation with the use of this decree is solved by the Committee for relations in between communities.

3. Article 69 of the Constitution of Republic of Macedonia is replaced by this amendment.

Amendment XI

This amendment is part of the Constitution of Republic of Macedonia and it is acting starting with the day of its proclamation 16th November 2001.

1. The Assembly chooses a national ombudsman with the majority of votes from the total number of representatives, while there has to be a majority of votes from the present representatives which belong to the communities that are not a majority in Republic of Macedonia.

2. The national ombudsman protects the constitutional and legal rights of the citizens which constitutional and legal rights are violated by the bodies of state government and from other bodies and organizations that have public authorizations. The national ombudsman pays special attention for protection of nondiscriminating principles appropriate and fair involvement of the representatives of the communities in the bodies of the state government, bodies of units of the local self-government and in the public institutions and services.

3. Paragraph 1 of article 77 of the Constitution of Republic of Macedonia is replaced by paragraph 1 of this amendment, and with paragraph 2 of this amendment, paragraph 2 of article 77 is supplemented.

Amendment XII

This amendment is part of the Constitution of Republic of Macedonia and it is acting starting with the day of its proclamation 16th November 2001.

1. The Assembly establishes a committee for relations between communities. The committee is conceited of 19 members out of which 7 from the Assembly representatives, Macedonians and Albanians and 1 from the Assembly representatives, Turks, Vlachs, Romas, Serbs and Bosnians. If one of the communities has no representatives, the national ombudsman, after consulting with the relevant representatives of those com-

munities, will propose the other members of the Committee. The Assembly chooses the members of the Committee. The Committee discusses about relations in between communities in the Republic and gives opinions and suggestions for their resolving. The Assembly is obliged to discuss the opinions and suggestions of the committee and to bring a decision about them. In case of controversy about the implementation of the procedure for voting in the Assembly, established in article 69 paragraph 2 the Committee decides, with majority votes from the members, if the procedure will be implemented.

2. With paragraph 1 of this amendment, article 78 is replaced, and paragraph 7 of article 84 from the Constitution of Republic of Macedonia is erased.

Amendment XIII

This amendment is part of the Constitution of Republic of Macedonia and it is acting starting with the day of its proclamation 16th November 2001.

1. While choosing the three members, the president will provide the contents of the Council, as a totality, to appropriately reflect the contents of the population in Republic of Macedonia.

2. With paragraph 1 of this amendment paragraph 2 of article 86 from the Constitution of Republic of Macedonia is supplemented.

Amendment XIV

This amendment is part of the Constitution of Republic of Macedonia and it is acting starting with the day of its proclamation 16th November 2001.

1. Three of the members are chosen of the majority votes from the total number of representatives, where they must be a majority votes of the total numbers of the representatives who belong to the communities which are not a majority in the Republic of Macedonia.

2. With this amendment paragraph 2 of article 104 of the Republic of Macedonia is supplemented.

Amendment XV

This amendment is part of the Constitution of Republic of Macedonia and it is acting starting with the day of its proclamation 16th November 2001.

1. The Assembly chooses the judges for the Constitutional Court. The Assembly chooses 6 judges of the Constitutional Court with the majority of votes of the total number of the representatives. The Assembly chooses 3 judges with the majority votes of the total number of representatives, while there have to be a majority votes of the total number of representatives who belong to the communities which are not a majority in the Republic of Macedonia. The mandate of the judges lasts for 9 years without any right of reelecting.
2. Paragraph 2 of article 109 of the Constitution of the Republic of Macedonia is replaced by this amendment.

Amendment XVI

This amendment is part of the Constitution of Republic of Macedonia and it is acting starting with the day of its proclamation 16th November 2001.

1. Local self-governing is regulated by law which is brought with 2/3 majority votes of the total number of representatives, while there have to be majority votes of the total number of the representatives which belong to the communities that are not a majority in the Republic of Macedonia. The laws for local financing, local elections, borders of the municipalities and for city Skopje, are brought with majority votes of the present representatives, while there has to be a majority of votes of the present representatives who belong to the communities which are not a majority of Republic of Macedonia.
2. Paragraph 5 of article 114 of the Constitution of the Republic of Macedonia is replaced by this amendment.

Amendment XVII

This amendment is part of the Constitution of Republic of Macedonia and it is acting starting with the day of its proclamation 16th November 2001.

1. In the units of the local self-governing the citizens directly and through out representatives participate in deciding about questions of local importance and especially in the areas of public services, urban infrastructure, rural planning, protection of environment, local economical development, local financing, communal activities, culture, sport, social and child protection, education, health protection and other areas established by law.

2. In city Skopje the citizens directly and through out representatives participate in deciding about issues of importance of the city Skopje, and especially in areas of public services, urban infrastructure and rural planning, protection of the environment, local economical development, local financing, communal activities, culture, sport, social and child protection, education, health protection and other areas established by law.

3. With paragraph 1 from this amendment paragraph 1 from article 115 of the Constitution of the Republic of Macedonia is replaced, and with paragraph 2, paragraph 2 of article 117 of the Constitution of the Republic of Macedonia is replaced.

Amendment XVIII

This amendment is part of the Constitution of Republic of Macedonia and it is acting starting with the day of its proclamation 16th November 2001.

1. Decision for changing the preamble, members of the local self-governing, article 131, whichever decree related to the rights of the members of the communities, especially including articles 7, 8, 9, 19, 48, 56, 69, 77, 78, 86, 104 and 109, as well as a decision for supplementing whichever new decree which is related to the subject of those decrees and those members, 2/3 majority of the total number of representatives will be needed, in which there have to be majority votes of the total number of representatives who belong to the communities which are not a majority in the Republic of Macedonia.

2. With this amendment a new paragraph 4 is added to article 131 of the Constitution of the Republic of Macedonia.

Appendix D

The Ohrid Framework Agreement

FRAMEWORK AGREEMENT

13.08.2001

The following points comprise an agreed framework for securing the future of Macedonia's democracy and permitting the development of closer and more integrated relations between the Republic of Macedonia and the Euro-Atlantic community. This Framework will promote the peaceful and harmonious development of civil society while respecting the ethnic identity and the interests of all Macedonian citizens.

1. Basic Principles

1.1. The use of violence in pursuit of political aims is rejected completely and unconditionally. Only peaceful political solutions can assure a stable and democratic future for Macedonia.

1.2. Macedonia's sovereignty and territorial integrity, and the unitary character of the State are inviolable and must be preserved. There are no territorial solutions to ethnic issues.

1.3. The multi-ethnic character of Macedonia's society must be preserved and reflected in public life.

1.4. A modern democratic state in its natural course of development and maturation must continually ensure that its Constitution fully meets the needs of all its citizens and comports with the highest international standards, which themselves continue to evolve.

1.5. The development of local self-government is essential for encouraging the participation of citizens in democratic life, and for promoting respect for the identity of communities.

2. Cessation of Hostilities

2.1. The parties underline the importance of the commitments of July 5, 2001. There shall be a complete cessation of hostilities, complete voluntary disarmament of the ethnic Albanian armed groups and their complete voluntary disbandment. They acknowledge that a decision by NATO to assist in this context will require the establishment of a general, unconditional and open-ended cease-fire, agreement on a political solution to the problems of this country, a clear commitment by the armed groups to voluntarily disarm, and acceptance by all the parties of the conditions and limitations under which the NATO forces will operate.

3. Development of Decentralized Government

3.1. A revised Law on Local Self-Government will be adopted that reinforces the powers of elected local officials and enlarges substantially their competencies in conformity with the Constitution (as amended in accordance with Annex A) and the European Charter on Local Self-Government, and reflecting the principle of subsidiarity in effect in the European Union. Enhanced competencies will relate principally to the areas of public services, urban and rural planning, environmental protection, local economic development, culture, local finances, education, social welfare, and health care. A law on financing of local self-government will be adopted to ensure an adequate system of financing to enable local governments to fulfill all of their responsibilities.

3.2. Boundaries of municipalities will be revised within one year of the completion of a new census, which will be conducted under international supervision by the end of 2001. The revision of the municipal boundaries will be effectuated by the local and national authorities with international participation.

3.3. In order to ensure that police are aware of and responsive to the needs and interests of the local population, local heads of police will be selected by municipal councils from lists of candidates proposed by the Ministry of Interior, and will communicate regularly with the councils. The Ministry of Interior will retain the authority to remove local heads of police in accordance with the law.

4. Non-Discrimination and Equitable Representation

4.1. The principle of non-discrimination and equal treatment of all under the law will be respected completely. This principle will be applied in particular with respect to employment in public administration and public enterprises, and access to public financing for business development.

4.2. Laws regulating employment in public administration will include measures to assure equitable representation of communities in all central and local public bodies and at all levels of employment within such bodies, while respecting the rules concerning competence and integrity that govern public administration. The authorities will take action to correct present imbalances in the composition of the public administration, in particular through the recruitment of members of under-represented communities. Particular attention will be given to ensuring as rapidly as possible that the police services will generally reflect the composition and distribution of the population of Macedonia, as specified in Annex C.

4.3. For the Constitutional Court, one-third of the judges will be chosen by the Assembly by a majority of the total number of Representatives that includes a majority of the total number of Representatives claiming to belong to the communities not in the majority in the population of Macedonia. This procedure also will apply to the election of the Ombudsman (Public Attorney) and the election of three of the members of the Judicial Council.

5. Special Parliamentary Procedures

5.1. On the central level, certain Constitutional amendments in accordance with Annex A and the Law on Local Self-Government cannot be approved without a qualified majority of two-thirds of votes, within which there must be a majority of the votes of Representatives claiming to belong to the communities not in the majority in the population of Macedonia.

5.2. Laws that directly affect culture, use of language, education, personal documentation, and use of symbols, as well as laws on local finances, local elections, the city of Skopje, and boundaries of municipalities must receive a majority of votes, within which there must be a majority of the votes of the Representatives claiming to belong to the communities not in the majority in the population of Macedonia.

6. Education and Use of Languages

6.1. With respect to primary and secondary education, instruction will be provided in the students' native languages, while at the same time uniform standards for academic programs will be applied throughout Macedonia.

6.2. State funding will be provided for university level education in languages spoken by at least 20 percent of the population of Macedonia, on the basis of specific agreements.

6.3. The principle of positive discrimination will be applied in the enrolment in State universities of candidates belonging to communities not in the majority in the population of Macedonia until the enrolment reflects equitably the composition of the population of Macedonia.

6.4. The official language throughout Macedonia and in the international relations of Macedonia is the Macedonian language.

6.5. Any other language spoken by at least 20 percent of the population is also an official language, as set forth herein. In the organs of the Republic of Macedonia, any official language other than Macedonian may be used in accordance with the law, as further elaborated in Annex B. Any person living in a unit of local self-government in which at least 20 percent of the population speaks an official language other than Macedonian may use any official language to communicate with the regional office of the central government with responsibility for that municipality; such an office will reply in that language in addition to Macedonian. Any person may use any official language to communicate with a main office of the central government, which will reply in that language in addition to Macedonian.

6.6. With respect to local self-government, in municipalities where a community comprises at least 20 percent of the population of the municipality, the language of that community will be used as an official language in addition to Macedonian. With respect to languages spoken by less than 20 percent of the population of the municipality, the local authorities will decide democratically on their use in public bodies.

6.7. In criminal and civil judicial proceedings at any level, an accused person or any party will have the right to translation at State expense of all proceedings as well as documents in accordance with relevant Council of Europe documents.

6.8. Any official personal documents of citizens speaking an official language other than Macedonian will also be issued in that language, in addition to the Macedonian language, in accordance with the law.

7. Expression of Identity

7.1. With respect to emblems, next to the emblem of the Republic of Macedonia, local authorities will be free to place on front of local public buildings emblems marking the identity of the community in the majority in the municipality, respecting international rules and usages.

8. Implementation

8.1. The Constitutional amendments attached at Annex A will be presented to the Assembly immediately. The parties will take all measures to assure adoption of these amendments within 45 days of signature of this Framework Agreement.

8.2. The legislative modifications identified in Annex B will be adopted in accordance with the timetables specified therein.

8.3. The parties invite the international community to convene at the earliest possible time a meeting of international donors that would address in particular macro-financial assistance; support for the financing of measures to be undertaken for the purpose of implementing this Framework Agreement, including measures to strengthen local self-government; and rehabilitation and reconstruction in areas affected by the fighting.

9. Annexes

The following Annexes constitute integral parts of this Framework Agreement:

A. Constitutional Amendments
B. Legislative Modifications
C. Implementation and Confidence-Building Measures

10. Final Provisions

10.1. This Agreement takes effect upon signature.

10.2. The English language version of this Agreement is the only authentic version.

10.3. This Agreement was concluded under the auspices of President Boris Trajkovski.

Done at Skopje, Macedonia on 13 August 2001, in the English language.

ANNEX A
CONSTITUTIONAL AMENDMENTS

Preamble

The citizens of the Republic of Macedonia, taking over responsibility for the present and future of their fatherland, aware and grateful to their predecessors for their sacrifice and dedication in their endeavors and struggle to create an independent and sovereign state of Macedonia, and responsible to future generations to preserve and develop everything that is valuable from the rich cultural inheritance and coexistence within Macedonia, equal in rights and obligations toward the common good—the Republic of Macedonia, in accordance with the tradition of the Kruševo Republic and the decisions of the Antifascist People's Liberation Assembly of Macedonia, and the Referendum of September 8, 1991, they have decided to establish the Republic of Macedonia as an independent, sovereign state, with the intention of establishing and consolidating rule of law, guaranteeing human rights and civil liberties, providing peace and coexistence, social justice, economic well-being and prosperity in the life of the individual and the community, and in this regard through their representatives in the Assembly of the Republic of Macedonia, elected in free and democratic elections, they adopt. . . .

Article 7

(1) The Macedonian language, written using its Cyrillic alphabet, is the official language throughout the Republic of Macedonia and in the international relations of the Republic of Macedonia.

(2) Any other language spoken by at least 20 percent of the population is also an official language, written using its alphabet, as specified below.

(3) Any official personal documents of citizens speaking an official language other than Macedonian shall also be issued in that language, in addition to the Macedonian language, in accordance with the law.

(4) Any person living in a unit of local self-government in which at least 20 percent of the population speaks an official language other than Macedonian may use any official language to communicate with the regional office of the central government with responsibility for that municipality; such an office shall reply in that language in addition to Macedonian. Any person may use any official language to communicate

with a main office of the central government, which shall reply in that language in addition to Macedonian.

(5) In the organs of the Republic of Macedonia, any official language other than Macedonian may be used in accordance with the law.

(6) In the units of local self-government where at least 20 percent of the population speaks a particular language, that language and its alphabet shall be used as an official language in addition to the Macedonian language and the Cyrillic alphabet. With respect to languages spoken by less than 20 percent of the population of a unit of local self-government, the local authorities shall decide on their use in public bodies.

Article 8

(1) The fundamental values of the constitutional order of the Republic of Macedonia are:

- the basic freedoms and rights of the individual and citizen, recognized in international law and set down in the Constitution;
- equitable representation of persons belonging to all communities in public bodies at all levels and in other areas of public life;

. . .

Article 19

(1) The freedom of religious confession is guaranteed.

(2) The right to express one's faith freely and publicly, individually or with others is guaranteed.

(3) The Macedonian Orthodox Church, the Islamic Religious Community in Macedonia, the Catholic Church, and other Religious communities and groups are separate from the state and equal before the law.

(4) The Macedonian Orthodox Church, the Islamic Religious Community in Macedonia, the Catholic Church, and other Religious communities and groups are free to establish schools and other social and charitable institutions, by ways of a procedure regulated by law.

Article 48

(1) Members of communities have a right freely to express, foster and develop their identity and community attributes, and to use their community symbols.

(2) The Republic guarantees the protection of the ethnic, cultural, linguistic and religious identity of all communities.

(3) Members of communities have the right to establish institutions for culture, art, science and education, as well as scholarly and other associations for the expression, fostering and development of their identity.

(4) Members of communities have the right to instruction in their language in primary and secondary education, as determined by law. In schools where education is carried out in another language, the Macedonian language is also studied.

Article 56

. . .

(2) The Republic guarantees the protection, promotion and enhancement of the historical and artistic heritage of Macedonia and all communities in Macedonia and the treasures of which it is composed, regardless of their legal status. The law regulates the mode and conditions under which specific items of general interest for the Republic can be ceded for use.

Article 69

. . .

(2) For laws that directly affect culture, use of language, education, personal documentation, and use of symbols, the Assembly makes decisions by a majority vote of the Representatives attending, within which there must be a majority of the votes of the Representatives attending who claim to belong to the communities not in the majority in the population of Macedonia. In the event of a dispute within the Assembly regarding the application of this provision, the Committee on Inter-Community Relations shall resolve the dispute.

Article 77

(1) The Assembly elects the Public Attorney by a majority vote of the total number of Representatives, within which there must be a majority of the votes of the total number of Representatives claiming to belong to the communities not in the majority in the population of Macedonia.

(2) The Public Attorney protects the constitutional rights and legal rights of citizens when violated by bodies of state administration and by other bodies and organizations with public mandates. The Public Attorney shall give particular attention to safeguarding the principles of non-discrimination and equitable representation of communities in public bodies at all levels and in other areas of public life.

. . .

Article 78

(1) The Assembly shall establish a Committee for Inter-Community Relations.

(2) The Committee consists of seven members each from the ranks of the Macedonians and Albanians within the Assembly, and five members from among the Turks, Vlachs, Romanies and two other communities. The five members each shall be from a different community; if fewer than five other communities are represented in the Assembly, the Public Attorney, after consultation with relevant community leaders, shall propose the remaining members from outside the Assembly.

(3) The Assembly elects the members of the Committee.

(4) The Committee considers issues of inter-community relations in the Republic and makes appraisals and proposals for their solution.

(5) The Assembly is obliged to take into consideration the appraisals and proposals of the Committee and to make decisions regarding them.

(6) In the event of a dispute among members of the Assembly regarding the application of the voting procedure specified in Article 69(2), the Committee shall decide by majority vote whether the procedure applies.

Article 84

The President of the Republic of Macedonia

. . .

~~proposes the members of the Council for Inter Ethnic Relations;~~(to be deleted). . . .

Article 86

(1) The President of the Republic is President of the Security Council of the Republic of Macedonia.

(2) The Security Council of the Republic is composed of the President of the Republic, the President of the Assembly, the Prime Minister, the Ministers heading the bodies of state administration in the fields of security, defence and foreign affairs and three members appointed by the President of the Republic. In appointing the three members, the President shall ensure that the Security Council as a whole equitably reflects the composition of the population of Macedonia.

(3) The Council considers issues relating to the security and defence of the Republic and makes policy proposals to the Assembly and the Government.

Article 104

(1) The Republican Judicial Council is composed of seven members.

(2) The Assembly elects the members of the Council. Three of the members shall be elected by a majority vote of the total number of Representatives, within which there must be a majority of the votes of the total number of Representatives claiming to belong to the communities not in the majority in the population of Macedonia.

. . .

Article 109

(1) The Constitutional Court of Macedonia is composed of nine judges.

(2) The Assembly elects six of the judges to the Constitutional Court by a majority vote of the total number of Representatives. The Assembly elects three of the judges by a majority vote of the total number of Representatives, within which there must be a majority of the votes of the total number of Representatives claiming to belong to the communities not in the majority in the population of Macedonia.

. . .

Article 114

. . .

(5) Local self-government is regulated by a law adopted by a two-thirds majority vote of the total number of Representatives, within which there must be a majority of the votes of the total number of Representatives claiming to belong to the communities not in the majority in the population of Macedonia. The laws on local finances, local elections, boundaries of municipalities, and the city of Skopje shall be adopted by a majority vote of the Representatives attending, within which there must be a majority of the votes of the Representatives attending who claim to belong to the communities not in the majority in the population of Macedonia.

Article 115

(1) In units of local self-government, citizens directly and through representatives participate in decision-making on issues of local relevance particularly in the fields of public services, urban and rural planning, environmental protection, local economic development, local finances, communal activities, culture, sport, social security and child care, education, health care and other fields determined by law.

. . .

Article 131

(1) The decision to initiate a change in the Constitution is made by the Assembly by a two-thirds majority vote of the total number of Representatives.

(2) The draft amendment to the Constitution is confirmed by the Assembly by a majority vote of the total number of Representatives and then submitted to public debate.

(3) The decision to change the Constitution is made by the Assembly by a two-thirds majority vote of the total number of Representatives.

(4) A decision to amend the Preamble, the articles on local self-government, Article 131, any provision relating to the rights of members of communities, including in particular Articles 7, 8, 9, 19, 48, 56, 69, 77, 78, 86, 104 and 109, as well as a decision to add any new provision relating to the subject matter of such provisions and articles, shall require a two-thirds majority vote of the total number of Representatives, within which there must be a majority of the votes of the total number of Representatives claiming to belong to the communities not in the majority in the population of Macedonia.

(5) The change in the Constitution is declared by the Assembly.

ANNEX B
LEGISLATIVE MODIFICATIONS

The parties will take all necessary measures to ensure the adoption of the legislative changes set forth hereafter within the time limits specified.

1. Law on Local Self-Government

The Assembly shall adopt within 45 days from the signing of the Framework Agreement a revised Law on Local Self-Government. This revised Law shall in no respect be less favorable to the units of local self-government and their autonomy than the draft Law proposed by the Government of the Republic of Macedonia in March 2001. The Law shall include competencies relating to the subject matters set forth in Section 3.1 of the Framework Agreement as additional independent competencies of the units of local self-government, and shall conform to Section 6.6 of the Framework Agreement. In addition, the Law shall provide that any State standards or procedures established in any laws concerning areas in which municipalities have independent competencies shall be limited to those which cannot be established as effectively at the local level; such laws shall further promote the municipalities' independent exercise of their competencies.

2. Law on Local Finance

The Assembly shall adopt by the end of the term of the present Assembly a law on local self-government finance to ensure that the units of local self-government have sufficient resources to carry out their tasks under the revised Law on Local Self-Government. In particular, the law shall:

- Enable and make responsible units of local self-government for raising a substantial amount of tax revenue;
- Provide for the transfer to the units of local self-government of a part of centrally raised taxes that corresponds to the functions of the units of local self-government and that takes account of the collection of taxes on their territories; and
- Ensure the budgetary autonomy and responsibility of the units of local self-government within their areas of competence.

3. Law on Municipal Boundaries

The Assembly shall adopt by the end of 2002 a revised law on municipal boundaries, taking into account the results of the census and the relevant guidelines set forth in the Law on Local Self-Government.

4. Laws Pertaining to Police Located in the Municipalities

The Assembly shall adopt before the end of the term of the present Assembly provisions ensuring:

- That each local head of the police is selected by the council of the municipality concerned from a list of not fewer than three candidates proposed by the Ministry of the Interior, among whom at least one candidate shall belong to the community in the majority in the municipality. In the event the municipal council fails to select any of the candidates proposed within 15 days, the Ministry of the Interior shall propose a second list of not fewer than three new candidates, among whom at least one candidate shall belong to the community in the majority in the municipality. If the municipal council again fails to select any of the candidates proposed within 15 days, the Minister of the Interior, after consultation with the Government, shall select the local head of police from among the two lists of candidates proposed by the Ministry of the Interior as well as three additional candidates proposed by the municipal council;

- That each local head of the police informs regularly and upon request the council of the municipality concerned;
- That a municipal council may make recommendations to the local head of police in areas including public security and traffic safety; and
- That a municipal council may adopt annually a report regarding matters of public safety, which shall be addressed to the Minister of the Interior and the Public Attorney (Ombudsman).

5. Laws on the Civil Service and Public Administration

The Assembly shall adopt by the end of the term of the present Assembly amendments to the laws on the civil service and public administration to ensure equitable representation of communities in accordance with Section 4.2 of the Framework Agreement.

6. Law on Electoral Districts

The Assembly shall adopt by the end of 2002 a revised Law on Electoral Districts, taking into account the results of the census and the principles set forth in the Law on the Election of Members for the Parliament of the Republic of Macedonia.

7. Rules of the Assembly

The Assembly shall amend by the end of the term of the present Assembly its Rules of Procedure to enable the use of the Albanian language in accordance with Section 6.5 of the Framework Agreement, paragraph 8 below, and the relevant amendments to the Constitution set forth in Annex A.

8. Laws Pertinent to the Use of Languages

The Assembly shall adopt by the end of the term of the present Assembly new legislation regulating the use of languages in the organs of the Republic of Macedonia. This legislation shall provide that:

- Representatives may address plenary sessions and working bodies of the Assembly in languages referred to in Article 7, paragraphs 1 and 2 of the Constitution (as amended in accordance with Annex A);

- Laws shall be published in the languages referred to in Article 7, paragraphs 1 and 2 of the Constitution (as amended in accordance with Annex A); and
- All public officials may write their names in the alphabet of any language referred to in Article 7, paragraphs 1 and 2 of the Constitution (as amended in accordance with Annex A) on any official documents.

The Assembly also shall adopt by the end of the term of the present Assembly new legislation on the issuance of personal documents.

The Assembly shall amend by the end of the term of the present Assembly all relevant laws to make their provisions on the use of languages fully compatible with Section 6 of the Framework Agreement.

9. Law on the Public Attorney

The Assembly shall amend by the end of 2002 the Law on the Public Attorney as well as the other relevant laws to ensure:

- That the Public Attorney shall undertake actions to safeguard the principles of non-discrimination and equitable representation of communities in public bodies at all levels and in other areas of public life, and that there are adequate resources and personnel within his office to enable him to carry out this function;
- That the Public Attorney establishes decentralized offices;
- That the budget of the Public Attorney is voted separately by the Assembly;
- That the Public Attorney shall present an annual report to the Assembly and, where appropriate, may upon request present reports to the councils of municipalities in which decentralized offices are established; and
- That the powers of the Public Attorney are enlarged:
- To grant to him access to and the opportunity to examine all official documents, it being understood that the Public Attorney and his staff will not disclose confidential information;
- To enable the Public Attorney to suspend, pending a decision of the competent court, the execution of an administrative act, if he determines that the act may result in an irreparable prejudice to the rights of the interested person; and
- To give to the Public Attorney the right to contest the conformity of laws with the Constitution before the Constitutional Court.

10. Other Laws

The Assembly shall enact all legislative provisions that may be necessary to give full effect to the Framework Agreement and amend or abrogate all provisions incompatible with the Framework Agreement.

ANNEX C
IMPLEMENTATION AND
CONFIDENCE-BUILDING MEASURES

1. International Support

1.1. The parties invite the international community to facilitate, monitor and assist in the implementation of the provisions of the Framework Agreement and its Annexes, and request such efforts to be coordinated by the EU in cooperation with the Stabilization and Association Council.

2. Census and Elections

2.1. The parties confirm the request for international supervision by the Council of Europe and the European Commission of a census to be conducted in October 2001.

2.2. Parliamentary elections will be held by 27 January 2002. International organizations, including the OSCE, will be invited to observe these elections.

3. Refugee Return, Rehabilitation and Reconstruction

3.1. All parties will work to ensure the return of refugees who are citizens or legal residents of Macedonia and displaced persons to their homes within the shortest possible timeframe, and invite the international community and in particular UNHCR to assist in these efforts.

3.2. The Government with the participation of the parties will complete an action plan within 30 days after the signature of the Framework Agreement for rehabilitation of and reconstruction in areas affected by the hostilities. The parties invite the international community to assist in the formulation and implementation of this plan.

3.3. The parties invite the European Commission and the World Bank to rapidly convene a meeting of international donors after adoption in the Assembly of the Constitutional amendments in Annex A and the revised Law on Local Self-Government to support the financing of measures to be undertaken for the purpose of implementing the Framework Agreement and its Annexes, including measures to strengthen local self-government and reform the police services, to address macro-financial assistance to the Republic of Macedonia, and to support the rehabilitation and reconstruction measures identified in the action plan identified in paragraph 3.2.

4. Development of Decentralized Government

4.1. The parties invite the international community to assist in the process of strengthening local self-government. The international community should in particular assist in preparing the necessary legal amendments related to financing mechanisms for strengthening the financial basis of municipalities and building their financial management capabilities, and in amending the law on the boundaries of municipalities.

5. Non-Discrimination and Equitable Representation

5.1. Taking into account the recommendations of the already established governmental commission, the parties will take concrete action to increase the representation of members of communities not in the majority in Macedonia in public administration, the military, and public enterprises, as well as to improve their access to public financing for business development.

5.2. The parties commit themselves to ensuring that the police services will by 2004 generally reflect the composition and distribution of the population of Macedonia. As initial steps toward this end, the parties commit to ensuring that 500 new police officers from communities not in the majority in the population of Macedonia will be hired and trained by July 2002, and that these officers will be deployed to the areas where such communities live. The parties further commit that 500 additional such officers will be hired and trained by July 2003, and that these officers will be deployed on a priority basis to the areas throughout Macedonia where such communities live. The parties invite the international community to support and assist with the implementation of these commitments, in particular through screening and selection of candidates and their training. The parties invite the OSCE, the European Union, and the United States to send an expert team as quickly as possible in order to assess how best to achieve these objectives.

5.3. The parties also invite the OSCE, the European Union, and the United States to increase training and assistance programs for police, including:

- professional, human rights, and other training;
- technical assistance for police reform, including assistance in screening, selection and promotion processes;

- development of a code of police conduct;
- cooperation with respect to transition planning for hiring and deployment of police officers from communities not in the majority in Macedonia; and
- deployment as soon as possible of international monitors and police advisors in sensitive areas, under appropriate arrangements with relevant authorities.

5.4. The parties invite the international community to assist in the training of lawyers, judges and prosecutors from members of communities not in the majority in Macedonia in order to be able to increase their representation in the judicial system.

6. Culture, Education and Use of Languages

6.1. The parties invite the international community, including the OSCE, to increase its assistance for projects in the area of media in order to further strengthen radio, TV and print media, including Albanian language and multiethnic media. The parties also invite the international community to increase professional media training programs for members of communities not in the majority in Macedonia. The parties also invite the OSCE to continue its efforts on projects designed to improve inter-ethnic relations.

6.2. The parties invite the international community to provide assistance for the implementation of the Framework Agreement in the area of higher education.

U.S. Department of State Press Release: "Ohrid, One Year After"

Press Statement
Philip T. Reeker, Deputy Spokesman
Washington, DC
13 August 2002

Anniversary of Ohrid Framework Agreement

Today marks the one-year anniversary of the signing of the Ohrid Framework Agreement, which laid a firm foundation for Macedonia's future peaceful development on the path of Euro-Atlantic integration. We recognize President Trajkovski and Macedonia's political leadership for the significant progress they have made in enacting Framework Agreement commitments, which have strengthened Macedonia's democracy by helping to meet the political aspirations of all its citizens. While important work remains for the next government, the Agreement's implementation is well-advanced and the groundwork for upcoming parliamentary elections has been accomplished.

Macedonia has much to be proud of: its political leaders and citizens made conscious and courageous decisions to reduce tensions, build bridges between ethnic communities, and reinforce the legal framework for the advancement of civil society within Macedonia. We call on all in Macedonia to support, contribute to, and build upon this momentum toward lasting peace, stability, and growth.

Macedonia's upcoming democratic elections must serve to solidify the gains made this past year. The world will be watching to see how Macedonia conducts these elections. We look to Macedonia's leaders to ensure that the elections are fair, free from violence, in conformity with international standards, and that the results are respected.

The United States, together with the European Union, our NATO Allies and OSCE partners, will continue to stand behind Macedonia, working with its democratically elected governments to support peace, the continued development of its democratic institutions, and its long-term economic renewal.

Released 13 August 2002

Index

About the Authors

P. H. LIOTTA is Professor of Humanities at Salve Regina University and Executive Director of the Pell Center for International Relations and Public Policy in Newport, Rhode Island. A former Fulbright scholar to Yugoslavia during its breakup as a nation-state, he has traveled extensively throughout the former Soviet Union, Central and Southwest Asia (including Iran), Europe, and the Balkan peninsula. The author of fifteen books, his recent work includes *The Uncertain Certainty: Human Security, Environmental Change, and the Future Euro-Mediterranean, Dismembering the State: The Death of Yugoslavia and Why It Matters* and *The Wolf at the Door: A Poetic Cycle Translated from the Macedonian of Bogomil Gjuzel.*

CINDY R. JEBB is a tenured Academy Professor and Director of Comparative Politics in the Department of Social Sciences at the United States Military Academy, West Point. She received her Ph.D. in Political Science from Duke University and served as a West Point Fellow at the United States Naval War College from 2000 to 2001. She is the author of *Bridging the Gap: Ethnicity, Legitimacy, and State Alignment in the International System.*